I0393680

U.S. Department of Justice
Office of Justice Programs
National Institute of Justice

**CBRN Protective Ensemble
Standard for Law Enforcement**

NIJ Standard-0116.00

November 2010

NCJ 221916

NATIONAL INSTITUTE OF JUSTICE

John H. Laub
Director

Ellen Scrivner
Deputy Director

John Morgan
Office Director, Office of Science and Technology

Davis Hart
Division Director, Operational Technologies Division

Debra Stoe
Physical Scientist, Operational Technologies Division

The preparation of this standard was sponsored by the National Institute of Justice.

The National Institute of Justice is a component of the Office of Justice Programs, which also includes the Bureau of Justice Assistance; the Bureau of Justice Statistics; the Community Capacity Development Office; the Office for Victims of Crime; the Office of Juvenile Justice and Delinquency Prevention; and the Office of Sex Offender Sentencing, Monitoring, Apprehending, Registering, and Tracking (SMART).

Special Technical Committee

This standard was developed by a Special Technical Committee of practitioners, technical experts and others with experience in standards development and conformity assessment. Committee members, their organizations and their professional affiliations are listed in Table 1 and Table 2.

Table 1. Practitioners

Type	Name	Organization	Professional Affiliation
Local (retired)	Edward Bailor, Chair	U.S. Capitol Police	Federal Bureau of Investigation National Academy, Fraternal Order of Police, Interagency Board, International Association of Chiefs of Police, National Sheriffs' Association, National Tactical Officers Association
Local	Edward Allen	Seminole County (Fla.) Sheriff's Department	National Tactical Officers Association
Local (former)	Mike Brown	National Sheriffs' Association	National Sheriffs' Association
Local (retired)	Martin Hutchings	Sacramento County (Calif.) Sheriff's Department	National Bomb Squad Commanders Advisory Board
Local	Heather McArthur	Phoenix (Ariz.) Police Department	
Local	Thomas Nolan	Upper Merion Township (Pa.) Police Department	National Tactical Officers Association
Local	Kevin M. Sommers	Warren (Mich.) Police Department	Fraternal Order of Police
State	David McBath	New York State Police	Interagency Board, International Association of Chiefs of Police
Federal	Hugh Breslin	U.S. Department of Homeland Security, Federal Law Enforcement Training Center	
Federal	Jerry Craig	U.S. Department of Justice, Drug Enforcement Administration	
Federal	Charles Onesko	U.S. Department of Justice, Federal Bureau of Investigation, Hazardous Materials Response Unit	

Table 2. Technical Experts and Others

Type	Name	Organization	Expertise
Federal	Stephanie Elder	U.S. Army Natick Soldier Research, Development and Engineering Center	Ergonomics and test methods
Federal	Gordon Gillerman	U.S. Department of Commerce, National Institute of Standards and Technology	Conformity assessment and standards
Federal	William Haskell	U.S. Department of Health and Human Services, National Institute for Occupational Safety and Health, National Personal Protective Technology Laboratory	Emergency Responder Personal Protective Equipment (PPE) performance criteria, test methods and standards
Federal	Gene Stark	U.S. Department of Defense, Joint Program Executive Office for Chemical and Biological Defense	Chemical and biological protection for military personnel
Federal	Elaine Stewart-Craig	U.S. Army Research, Development and Engineering Command, Edgewood Chemical Biological Center	Chemical and biological protection for military personnel
Private	Steven Corrado	Underwriters Laboratories Inc.	Certification, compliance testing and standards
Private	Patricia Gleason	Safety Equipment Institute	Certification, testing and standards
Private	Thomas Neal	Neal Associates Ltd.	Standards and test methods
Private	Bruce Teele	National Fire Protection Association	Standards

Advisory Working Group

The work of the Special Technical Committee was reviewed by an Advisory Working Group (AWG) made up of senior-level representatives from stakeholder organizations and individuals with experience in standards development and conformity assessment. Organizations represented on the AWG are listed in Table 3 below.

Table 3. AWG Members

Organization
U.S. Department of Homeland Security, Science and Technology Directorate
Fraternal Order of Police
National Tactical Officers Association
U.S. Department of Homeland Security, Office for State and Local Law Enforcement
InterAgency Board for Equipment Standardization and Interoperability
International Association of Chiefs of Police, Center for Police Leadership
National Sheriffs' Association
National Fire Protection Association

Steering Committee

The Steering Committee generally directed the effort and helped to ensure coordination among relevant federal programs. Members of the Steering Committee and their organizations are listed in Table 4 below.

Table 4. Steering Committee Members

Member	Organization	Title
John Morgan, Chair	U.S. Department of Justice, Office of Justice Programs, National Institute of Justice	Director for Science and Technology
Bert Coursey	U.S. Department of Homeland Security, Science and Technology Directorate, Office of Standards	Director
Mark Stolorow	U.S. Department of Commerce, National Institute of Standards and Technology, Office of Law Enforcement Standards	Director

FOREWORD

This document is a voluntary performance standard for chemical, biological, radiological and nuclear (CBRN) protective ensembles for use by law enforcement. It defines both performance requirements and the methods used to test performance. In order for an ensemble manufacturer or other entity to claim that a particular CBRN protective ensemble model satisfies this National Institute of Justice (NIJ) standard, the model must be in compliance with this standard as determined in accordance with this document and the associated document, *Law Enforcement CBRN Protective Ensemble Certification Program Requirements,* NIJ CR-0116.00. Both this standard and the associated certification program requirements document are produced as a part of the Standards and Testing Program of the U.S. Department of Justice, Office of Justice Programs, NIJ, as is a third associated document, the *Law Enforcement CBRN Protective Ensemble Selection and Application Guide,* NIJ Guide-0116.00.

All requirements stated in this standard, including those that explicitly employ mandatory language (e.g., "shall") are those necessary to satisfy the standard. Nothing in this document is intended to require or imply that commercially available CBRN protective ensembles for use by law enforcement must satisfy this standard.

This document is a performance and testing standard and, therefore, provides precise and detailed test methods. Portions of this standard are used with permission from the National Fire Protection Association (NFPA), and references to the NFPA documents listed below are cited throughout the text using letter symbols as indicated in Table 5 on page xv:

NFPA 1994, *Standard on Protective Ensembles for First Responders to CBRN Terrorism Incidents,* copyright 2007, National Fire Protection Association, Quincy, MA. All rights reserved under the copyright laws of the United States; such material is not to be considered in the public domain.

NFPA 1951, *Standard on Protective Ensembles for Technical Rescue Operations,* copyright 2007, National Fire Protection Association, Quincy, MA. All rights reserved under the copyright laws of the United States; such material is not to be considered in the public domain.

NFPA 1971, *Standard on Protective Ensembles for Structural Fire Fighting and Proximity Fire Fighting,* copyright 2007, National Fire Protection Association, Quincy, MA. All rights reserved under the copyright laws of the United States; such material is not to be considered in the public domain.

NFPA 1991, *Standard on Vapor-Protective Ensembles for Hazardous Materials Emergencies,* copyright 2005, National Fire Protection Association, Quincy, MA. All rights reserved under the copyright laws of the United States; such material is not to be considered in the public domain.

Portions of this standard are derived from documents generated by the U.S. Army Natick Soldier Research, Development and Engineering Center, National Protection Center. References to the documents listed below are cited throughout the text using letter symbols as indicated in Table 5, page xv:

Gaps Analysis Report of Chemical/Biological Protective Ensembles for the Law Enforcement Advanced Protection (LEAP) Program. 2008. Natick, MA: Commander, U.S. Army Research, Development and Engineering Command, Soldier Systems Center, Natick Soldier Research, Development and Engineering Center, National Protection Center.

Proposed Specifications for a Performance Standard for Chemical and Biological Protective Clothing and Equipment for Law Enforcement Operations. 2008. Natick, MA: Commander, U.S. Army Research, Development and Engineering Command, Soldier Systems Center, Natick Soldier Research, Development and Engineering Center, National Protection Center.

NIJ standards are subject to continued research, development and testing, and to review and modification as appropriate on an ongoing basis. Users of this standard are advised to check with http://www.justnet.org on a regular basis to determine whether it has been revised or superseded.

Technical comments and recommended revisions are welcome. Please send all written comments and suggestions to Director, National Institute of Justice, Office of Justice Programs, U.S. Department of Justice, 810 Seventh St., N.W., Washington, DC, 20531.

Nothing in this document is intended to create any legal or procedural rights enforceable against the United States. Moreover, nothing in this document creates any obligation for manufacturers, law enforcement agencies or others to follow or adopt this voluntary law enforcement technology equipment standard.

CONTENTS

ABBREVIATIONS, SYMBOLS, PREFIXES AND CONVERSIONS

Standard-Specific Abbreviations

APR	Air Purifying Respirator
CAS	Chemical Abstracts Registry
CBRN	Chemical, Biological, Radiological, Nuclear
CEN	European Committee for Standardization
C.F.R.	Code of Federal Regulations
CWA	Chemical Warfare Agent
dBA	Decibels Adjusted
DHS	U.S. Department of Homeland Security
DOJ	U.S. Department of Justice
FR	Flame-resistant
IDLH	Immediately Dangerous to Life and Health
LERL	Law Enforcement Response Level
LPM	Liters Per Minute
MeS	Methyl Salicylate
MIST	Man-in-Simulant Test
NFPA	National Fire Protection Association
NLECTC	National Law Enforcement and Corrections Technology Center
NIJ	National Institute of Justice, U.S. Department of Justice
NIOSH	National Institute for Occupational Safety and Health, U.S. Department of Health and Human Services
NIST	National Institute of Standards and Technology, U.S. Department of Commerce
OLES	Office of Law Enforcement Standards, U.S. Department of Commerce
OSHA	Occupational Safety and Health Administration, U.S. Department of Labor
PAD	Passive Absorbent Dosimeter
PAPR	Powered Air Purifying Respirator
PPDF	Physiological Protective Dosage Factor
PPE	Personal Protective Equipment
SCBA	Self-Contained Breathing Apparatus
TEP	Triethyl phosphate
TIC	Toxic Industrial Chemical
TOP	Test Operations Procedure
VFS	Visual Field Score

COMMONLY USED SYMBOLS AND ABBREVIATIONS

A	ampere	H	Henry	nm	nanometer
ac	alternating current	h	Hour	No.	number
AM	amplitude modulation	hf	high frequency	o.d.	outside diameter
cd	candela	Hz	Hertz	Ω	ohm
cm	centimeter	i.d.	inside diameter	p.	page
CP	chemically pure	in	inch	Pa	pascal
c/s	cycle per second	IR	infrared	pe	probable error
d	day	J	joule	pp.	pages
dB	decibel	L	lambert	ppm	parts per million
dc	direct current	L	liter	qt	quart
°C	degree Celsius	Lb	pound	rad	radian
°F	degree Fahrenheit	lbf	pound force	rf	radio frequency
diam	diameter	lbf·in	pound force inch	RH	relative humidity
emf	electromotive force	lm	lumen	s	second
eq	equation	ln	logarithm (base e)	SD	standard deviation
F	farad	log	logarithm (base 10)	sec.	section
fc	footcandle	M	molar	SWR	standing wave ratio
fig.	figure	m	meter	uhf	ultrahigh frequency
FM	frequency modulation	min.	minute	UV	ultraviolet
ft	foot	mm	millimeter	V	volt
ft/s	foot per second	mph	miles per hour	vhf	very high frequency
g	acceleration	m/s	meter per second	W	watt
g	gram	N	newton	λ	wavelength
gr	grain	N·m	newton meter	wt	weight

area = unit^2 (e.g., ft^2, in^2, etc.); volume = unit^3 (e.g., ft^3, m^3, etc.)

PREFIXES

d	deci (10^{-1})	da	deka (10)
c	centi (10^{-2})	h	hecto (10^2)
m	milli (10^{-3})	k	kilo (10^3)
μ	micro (10^{-6})	M	mega (10^6)
n	nano (10^{-9})	G	giga (10^9)
p	pico (10^{-12})	T	tera (10^{12})

COMMON CONVERSIONS

0.30480 m = 1 ft	4.448222 N = 1 lbf
2.54 cm = 1 in	1.355818 J = 1 ft·lbf
0.4535924 kg = 1 lb	0.1129848 N.m = 1 lbf·in
0.06479891 g = 1 gr	14.59390 N/m = 1 lbf/ft
0.9463529 L = 1 qt	6894.757 Pa = 1 lbf/in^2
3600000 J = 1 kW·h	1.609344 km/h = 1 mph

Notice

Portions of this standard are derived from NFPA standards (used with permission) and documents of the U.S. Army Research, Development and Engineering Command, Soldier Systems Center, Natick Soldier Research, Development and Engineering Center. References to these documents are cited throughout the text using superscripted letter symbols as indicated in Table 5 below:

Table 5. Referenced Standards and Symbols for Citation

Symbol for Citation	Cited Standards and Publications
A	NFPA 1994, *Standard on Protective Ensembles for First Responders to CBRN Terrorism Incidents,* copyright 2007, National Fire Protection Association, Quincy, MA. All rights are reserved under the copyright laws of the United States; such material is not to be considered in the public domain.
B	NFPA 1971, *Standard on Protective Ensembles for Structural Fire Fighting and Proximity Fire Fighting,* copyright 2007, National Fire Protection Association, Quincy, MA. All rights are reserved under the copyright laws of the United States; such material is not to be considered in the public domain.
C	NFPA 1951, *Standard on Protective Ensembles for Technical Rescue Operations,* copyright 2007, National Fire Protection Association, Quincy, MA. All rights are reserved under the copyright laws of the United States; such material is not to be considered in the public domain.
D	NFPA 1991, *Standard on Vapor-Protective Ensembles for Hazardous Materials Emergencies,* copyright 2005, National Fire Protection Association, Quincy, MA. All rights are reserved under the copyright laws of the United States; such material is not to be considered in the public domain.
E	*Gaps Analysis Report of Chemical/Biological Protective Ensembles for the Law Enforcement Advanced Protection (LEAP) Program.* 2008. Natick, MA: Commander, U.S. Army Research, Development and Engineering Command, Soldier Systems Center, Natick Soldier Research, Development and Engineering Center, National Protection Center.
F	*Proposed Specifications for a Performance Standard for Chemical and Biological Protective Clothing and Equipment for Law Enforcement Operations.* 2008. Natick, MA: Commander, U.S. Army Research, Development and Engineering Command, Soldier Systems Center, Natick Soldier Research, Development and Engineering Center, National Protection Center.

1. SCOPE, PURPOSE AND APPLICATION

1.1 Scope

1.1.1 This document is a voluntary standard. All requirements stated in this standard, including those that explicitly employ mandatory language (e.g., "shall") are those necessary to satisfy the standard. Nothing in this document is intended to require or imply that commercially available chemical, biological, radiological and nuclear (CBRN) protective ensembles for use by law enforcement must satisfy this standard. In order for an ensemble manufacturer or other entity to claim that a particular CBRN protective ensemble model satisfies this NIJ standard, however, the model must be found to comply with this standard as determined in accordance with this document and the associated document, *Law Enforcement CBRN Protective Ensemble Certification Program Requirements,* NIJ CR-0116.00.

1.1.2 This standard specifies the minimum requirements for form and fit, performance, testing, documentation and labeling of CBRN protective ensembles intended to protect law enforcement personnel from CBRN hazards. CBRN hazards include chemical warfare agents (CWAs), toxic industrial chemicals (TICs), biological agents and radiological and nuclear particulate hazards that may inflict bodily harm, incapacitation or death.[A]

1.1.3 CBRN protective ensembles consist of four elements:

- Garment covering the wearer's upper and lower torso, arms, legs and head.
- Hand protection elements covering the wearer's wrists and hands.
- Foot protection covering the wearer's feet, ankles and lower legs.
- Respiratory protection.

Figure 1 provides a pictorial representation of a CBRN protective ensemble and its elements.

Figure 1. CBRN Protective Ensemble and Its Elements

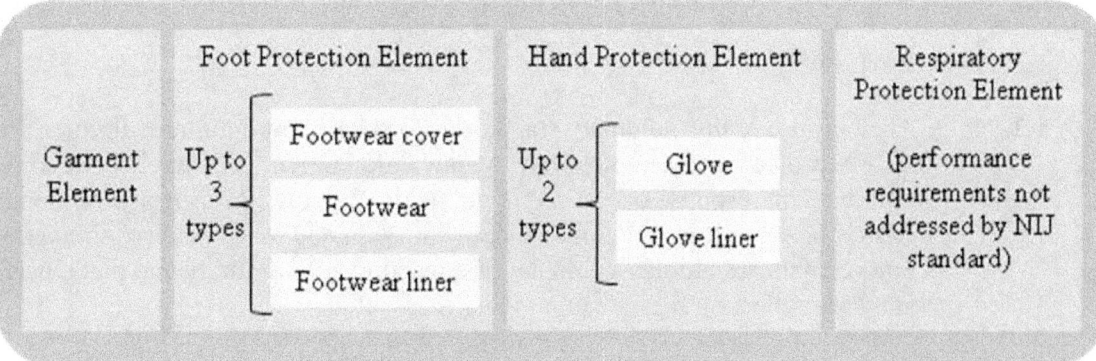

1.1.4 Although respiratory protection is a CBRN protective ensemble element, performance requirements for respiratory protection are addressed in other, non-NIJ standards and are not addressed in this standard. Requirements in this standard address the CBRN protective ensemble overall and three of the elements (excluding respiratory protection).

1.1.5 This standard specifies requirements for new, unworn law enforcement CBRN protective ensembles and ensemble elements.

1.1.6 This standard does not specify requirements for protection from ballistic threats, explosives or ionizing radiation.

1.1.7 This standard does not apply to any accessories, and all testing required in this standard shall be performed with no accessories attached. (See 3.2.1, Accessories.)

1.1.8 This standard shall not be understood as addressing all of the safety concerns associated with the use of CBRN protective ensembles and ensemble elements. Users of this standard should be aware of all safety and health issues associated with the use of CBRN protective ensembles. User information related to these issues is provided in *Law Enforcement CBRN Protective Ensemble Selection and Application Guide,* NIJ Guide-0116.00.

1.1.9 This standard shall not be understood as addressing the safety concerns, if any, associated with the use of this standard by testing facilities.

1.1.10 No ensemble manufacturer or other entity shall claim compliance with only selected portions of this standard. The CBRN protective ensemble model shall meet all applicable stated requirements.

1.1.11 Nothing herein shall be understood to restrict any ensemble manufacturer from exceeding the requirements of this standard.

1.1.12 As appropriate (e.g., for models that employ materials or forms of construction that were not anticipated when this standard was developed or are not addressed by this standard), NIJ may modify the test methods of the standard or establish new ones.

1.2 **Purpose**

1.2.1 The purpose of this voluntary standard is to specify minimum requirements for CBRN protective ensembles worn by law enforcement personnel conducting law enforcement response operations at an incident involving suspected or identified CBRN hazards. It is recognized that the mission and associated requirements of law enforcement are unique within the first responder community and that a performance standard reflecting these requirements is essential.

1.2.2   The purpose of the test methods in this standard is to assess performance and should not be understood to specify performance levels for all situations and hazards to which law enforcement personnel may be exposed.

1.3   Application

1.3.1   This standard provides for four levels of CBRN protective ensembles that could be selected for protection of law enforcement personnel. The four levels are based on mission requirements, expected mission duration, durability requirements of different operations and activities, and hazards in the CBRN threat environments.

1.3.2   The requirements for Law Enforcement Response Level 1 (LERL-1) CBRN protective ensemble models and ensemble elements apply to ensemble models and ensemble elements intended to provide limited protection to law enforcement personnel making tactical entry into environments involving CBRN hazards, conditions in which contaminant concentrations are unknown or are known to be at or above immediately dangerous to life and health (IDLH) levels requiring the use of a self-contained breathing apparatus (SCBA), and flame and flash fire hazards. LERL-1 ensembles are intended to withstand the rigorous use associated with tactical operations. These ensemble models are required to be tested against two CWAs and 24 TICs that are representative of many chemical threats.

1.3.3   The requirements for Law Enforcement Response Level 2 (LERL-2) CBRN protective ensemble models and ensemble elements apply to ensemble models and ensemble elements intended to provide limited protection to law enforcement personnel making tactical entry into environments involving CBRN hazards and conditions in which contaminant concentrations are unknown or are known to be at or above IDLH levels requiring the use of an SCBA. LERL-2 ensembles are intended to withstand the rigorous use associated with tactical operations. These ensemble models are required to be tested against the same two CWAs as LERL-1 ensemble models and five TICs.

1.3.4   The requirements for Law Enforcement Response Level 3 (LERL-3) CBRN protective ensemble models and ensemble elements apply to ensemble models and ensemble elements intended to provide limited protection to law enforcement personnel making tactical entry into environments involving CBRN hazards and conditions in which contaminant concentrations are known to be below IDLH levels permitting the use of an air purifying respirator (APR) or powered APR (PAPR). LERL-3 ensembles are intended to withstand the rigorous use associated with tactical operations. These ensemble models are required to be tested against the same CWAs and TICs as LERL-2 ensemble models.

1.3.5   The requirements for Law Enforcement Response Level 4 (LERL-4) CBRN protective ensemble models and ensemble elements apply to ensemble models and ensemble elements intended to provide limited protection to law enforcement personnel performing perimeter operations at incidents involving CBRN hazards and conditions in which contaminant concentrations are known to be below IDLH levels permitting the use of an APR or PAPR and where mission tasks require less stringent ensemble durability. These ensemble models are required to be tested against the same CWAs and TICs as LERL-2 and LERL-3 ensemble models.

1.4   Units

1.4.1   In this standard, values for measurement are followed by an approximate equivalent in parentheses, but only the first stated value shall be regarded as the requirement.[A]

2.   REFERENCES

2.1   Associated Publications

The following document is a companion publication to NIJ Standard-0116.00 and NIJ CR-0116.00.

NIJ Guide-0116.00, *Law Enforcement CBRN Protective Ensemble Selection and Application Guide*. Washington, DC: National Institute of Justice, U.S. Department of Justice.

2.2   Referenced Publications

The following references form a basis for and provide support for the requirements and procedures described in this standard. For dated references, only the edition cited applies. For undated references, the latest edition of the referenced document applies, including any amendments.

2.2.1   ASTM International Publications

ASTM Standard D123, 2007, "Standard Terminology Relating to Textiles," ASTM International, West Conshohocken, PA, 2007, www.astm.org.

ASTM Standard D1424, 2007, "Standard Test Method for Tearing Strength of Fabrics by Falling—Pendulum Type (Elmendorf) Apparatus," ASTM International, West Conshohocken, PA, 2007, DOI: 10.1520/D1424-07, www.astm.org.

ASTM Standard D1630, 2006, "Standard Test Method for Rubber Property-Abrasion Resistance (Footwear Abrader)," ASTM International, West Conshohocken, PA, 2006, DOI: 10.1520/D1630-06, www.astm.org.

ASTM Standard D1683, 2007, "Standard Test Method for Failure in Sewn Seams of Woven Apparel Fabrics," ASTM International, West Conshohocken, PA, 2007, DOI: 10.1520/D1683-07, www.astm.org.

ASTM Standard D1776, 2004, "Standard Practice for Conditioning and Testing Textiles," ASTM International, West Conshohocken, PA, 2004, DOI: 10.1520/D1776-08E01, www.astm.org.

ASTM Standard D2136, 2002, "Standard Test Method for Coated Fabrics—Low Temperature Bend Test," ASTM International, West Conshohocken, PA, 2002, DOI: 10.1520/D2136-02, www.astm.org.

ASTM Standard D3787, 2007, "Standard Test Method for Bursting Strength of Textiles—Constant-Rate-of-Traverse (CRT) Ball Burst Test," ASTM International, West Conshohocken, PA, 2007, DOI: 10.1520/D3787-07, www.astm.org.

ASTM Standard D4157, 2007, "Standard Test Method for Abrasion Resistance of Textile Fabrics (Oscillatory Cylinder Method)," ASTM International, West Conshohocken, PA, 2007, DOI: 10.1520/D4157-07, www.astm.org.

ASTM Standard D6413, 2008, "Standard Test Method for Flame Resistance of Textiles (Vertical Test)," ASTM International, West Conshohocken, PA, 2008, DOI: 10.1520/D6413, www.astm.org.

ASTM Standard F392, 2004, "Standard Test Method for Flex Durability of Flexible Barrier Materials," ASTM International, West Conshohocken, PA, 2004, DOI: 10.1520/F0392-93R04, www.astm.org.

ASTM Standard F489, 1996, "Standard Test Method for Static Coefficient of Friction of Shoe Sole and Heel Material as Measured by the James Machine," ASTM International, West Conshohocken, PA, 1996, DOI: 10.1520/F0489-96E01, www.astm.org.

ASTM Standard F739, 1999, "Standard Test Method for Resistance of Protective Clothing Materials to Permeation by Liquids or Gases Under Conditions of Continuous Contact," ASTM International, West Conshohocken, PA, 1999, DOI: 10.1520/F0739-99A, www.astm.org.

ASTM Standard F1342, 1996, "Standard Test Method for Resistance of Protective Clothing Materials to Puncture," ASTM International, West Conshohocken, PA, 1996, DOI: 10.1520/F1342-91R96E02, www.astm.org.

ASTM Standard F1358, 2008, "Standard Test Method for Effects of Flame Impingement on Materials Used In Protective Clothing Not Designated Primarily for Flame Resistance," ASTM International, West Conshohocken, PA, 2008, DOI: 10.1520/F1358-08, www.astm.org.

ASTM Standard F1359, 2004, "Standard Test Method for Measuring the Liquid Permeation Resistance of Protective Clothing or Protective Ensembles Under a Shower Spray While on a Mannequin," ASTM International, West Conshohocken, PA, 2004, DOI: 10.1520/F1359-99AR04, www.astm.org.

ASTM Standard F1671, 2003, "Standard Test Method for Resistance of Materials Used in Protective Clothing to Penetration by Blood-Borne Pathogens Using Phi-X174 Bacteriophage as a Test System," ASTM International, West Conshohocken, PA, 2003, DOI: 10.1520/F1671-03, www.astm.org.

ASTM Standard F1790, 2004, "Standard Test Methods for Measuring Cut Resistance of Materials Used in Protective Clothing," ASTM International, West Conshohocken, PA, 2004, DOI: 10.1520/F1790-04, www.astm.org.

ASTM Standard F1868, 2002, "Standard Test Method for Thermal and Evaporative Resistance of Clothing Materials Using a Sweating Hot Plate," ASTM International, West Conshohocken, PA, 2002, DOI: 10.1520/F1868-02, www.astm.org.

ASTM Standard F1930, 2000, "Standard Test Method for Evaluation of Flame Resistant Clothing for Protection Against Flash Fire Simulations Using an Instrumented Manikin," ASTM International, West Conshohocken, PA, 2000, DOI: 10.1520/F1930-00R08, www.astm.org.

ASTM Standard F2588, 2007, "Standard Test Method for Man-In-Simulant Test (MIST) for Protective Ensembles," ASTM International, West Conshohocken, PA, 2007, DOI: 10.1520/F2588-07, www.astm.org.

2.2.2   Code of Federal Regulations

29 C.F.R. Part 1910, Subpart I (Personal Protective Equipment).

29 C.F.R. § 1910.120 (Hazardous Waste Operations and Emergency Response).

29 C.F.R. § 1910.1030 (Bloodborne Pathogens).

42 C.F.R. Part 84 (Approval of Respiratory Protective Devices).

2.2.3   European Standards

EN 136, *Respiratory Protective Devices – Full Face Masks – Requirements, Testing, Marking.* 1998. Brussels, Belgium: European Committee for Standardization.

EN 420, *Protective Gloves – General Requirements and Test Methods.* 2003. Brussels, Belgium: European Committee for Standardization.

IEC 61672-1, *International Standard – Electroacoustics – Sound Level Meters – Part 1: Specifications.* 2002. Geneva, Switzerland: International Electrotechnical Commission.

2.2.4   NFPA Publications

NFPA 1951, *Standard on Protective Ensembles for Technical Rescue Operations.* 2007. Quincy, MA: National Fire Protection Association.

NFPA 1971, *Standard on Protective Ensembles for Structural Fire Fighting and Proximity Fire Fighting.* 2007. Quincy, MA: National Fire Protection Association.

NFPA 1975, *Standard on Station/Work Uniforms for Fire and Emergency Services.* 2004. Quincy, MA: National Fire Protection Association.

NFPA 1981, *Standard on Open-Circuit Self-Contained Breathing Apparatus (SCBA) for Emergency Services.* 2007. Quincy, MA: National Fire Protection Association.

NFPA 1991, *Standard on Vapor-Protective Ensembles for Hazardous Materials Emergencies.* 2005. Quincy, MA: National Fire Protection Association.

NFPA 1992, *Standard on Liquid Splash-Protective Ensembles and Clothing for Hazardous Materials Emergencies.* 2005. Quincy, MA: National Fire Protection Association.

NFPA 1994, *Standard on Protective Ensembles for First Responders to CBRN Terrorism Incidents.* 2007. Quincy, MA: National Fire Protection Association.

NFPA 1999, *Standard on Protective Clothing for Emergency Medical Operations.* 2003. Quincy, MA: National Fire Protection Association.

NFPA 2112, *Standard on Flame-Resistant Garments for Protection of Industrial Personnel Against Flash Fire.* 2007. Quincy, MA: National Fire Protection Association.

2.2.5   U.S. Department of Health and Human Services Publications

NIOSH Procedure No. CET-APRS-STP-CBRN-0312, *Determination of Field of View for Full Facepiece Chemical Biological Radiological Nuclear (CBRN) Respiratory Protective Devices (RPD).* 2005. Washington, DC: National Institute for Occupational Safety and Health, U.S. Department of Health and Human Services.

NIOSH Publication No. 2008-132, *Attention Emergency Responders: Responders Guidance on Emergency Responder Personal Protective Equipment (PPE) for Response to CBRN Terrorism Incidents,* 2008. Washington, DC: National Institute for Occupational Safety and Health, U.S. Department of Health and Human Services

NIOSH Statement of Standard for CBRN Full Facepiece Air Purifying Respirators (APR). 2003. Washington, DC: National Institute for Occupational Safety and Health, U.S. Department of Health and Human Services.

NIOSH Statement of Standard for CBRN Open Circuit Self-Contained Breathing Apparatus (SCBA). 2002. Washington, DC: National Institute for Occupational Safety and Health, U.S. Department of Health and Human Services.

NIOSH Statement of Standard for CBRN Powered Air-Purifying Respirator (PAPR). 2006. Washington, DC: National Institute for Occupational Safety and Health, U.S. Department of Health and Human Services.

2.2.6   U.S. Department of Justice

NIJ Standard-0101.06, *Ballistic Resistance of Body Armor.* Washington, DC: National Institute of Justice, U.S. Department of Justice.

NIJ CR-0116.00, *Law Enforcement CBRN Protective Ensemble Certification Program Requirements*. Washington, DC: National Institute of Justice, U.S. Department of Justice.

2.2.7   U.S. Military Publications

MIL-STD-810E, *Environmental Test Methods and Engineering Guidelines*. 1989. Washington, DC: U.S. Department of Defense.

MIL-STD-810F, *Test Method Standard for Environmental Engineering Considerations and Laboratory Tests*. 2000. Washington, DC: U.S. Department of Defense.

Test Operations Procedure (TOP) 8-2-501, *Permeation and Penetration Testing of Air-Permeable, Semipermeable, and Impermeable Materials with Chemical Agents or Simulants (Swatch Testing)*. 2002. Aberdeen Proving Ground, MD: U.S. Army Developmental Test Command.

TOP 10-2-022, *Chemical Vapor and Aerosol System Level Testing of Chemical/Biological Protective Suits*. 2001. Aberdeen Proving Ground, MD: U.S. Army Developmental Test Command.

Gaps Analysis Report of Chemical/Biological Protective Ensembles for the Law Enforcement Advanced Protection (LEAP) Program. 2008. Natick, MA: Commander, U.S. Army Research, Development and Engineering Command, Soldier Systems Center, Natick Soldier Research, Development and Engineering Center, National Protection Center.

Proposed Specifications for a Performance Standard for Chemical and Biological Protective Clothing and Equipment for Law Enforcement Operations. 2008. Natick, MA: Commander, U.S. Army Research, Development and Engineering Command, Soldier Systems Center, Natick Soldier Research, Development and Engineering Center, National Protection Center.

2.2.8   Other Industry Publications

AATCC Evaluation Procedure 6. 2008. Research Triangle Park, NC: The American Association of Textile Chemists and Colorists.

American Medical Association Guides to the Evaluation of Permanent Impairment, 5th edition. 2000. Chicago, IL: American Medical Association.

FIA 1209, *Whole Shoe Flex*. 1984. Washington, DC: Footwear Industries of America.

3. DEFINITIONS

3.1 General

The definitions contained in this chapter shall apply to these terms as used in this standard. Where terms are not defined in this chapter or within another chapter, they shall be defined using their ordinarily accepted meanings, unless the context unmistakably indicates otherwise.

3.2 Definitions

3.2.1   **Accessories:** Any ensemble manufacturer-recommended or aftermarket items that can be attached to the CBRN protective ensemble but that are not necessary for meeting the requirements of this standard.

3.2.2   **Ballistic body armor:** Personal protective equipment that provides protection against specific ballistic threats within its coverage area, which is typically the torso.

3.2.3   **Biological agents:** Liquid or particulate agents that consist of a biologically derived toxin or pathogen used to inflict lethal or incapacitating casualties. [A]

3.2.4   **Bloodborne pathogens:** Pathogenic microorganisms present in human blood that can cause disease in humans. Examples of pathogens include hepatitis B virus (HBV), hepatitis C virus (HCV) and human immunodeficiency virus (HIV). (See, e.g., 29 C.F.R. § 1910.1030 (b).)

3.2.5   **Care:** Cleaning, decontamination and storage of a product.

3.2.6   **CBRN:** An abbreviation for chemical, biological, radiological and nuclear.

3.2.7   **CBRN protective ensembles:** Equipment intended to provide limited full-body protection against exposure to CBRN hazards. (See 1.3.2 through 1.3.5.)

3.2.8   **Chemical warfare agents (CWA):** Mainly liquid, but also solid, gaseous and vaporous chemical substances traditionally used during warfare or armed conflict to kill or incapacitate an enemy or to inflict lethal or incapacitating casualties. [A]

3.2.9   **Closure:** A component intended and configured to allow the wearer to don and doff the CBRN protective ensemble. [A]

3.2.10   **Closure assembly:** A combination of the closure and the seam attaching the closure to the ensemble, including any protective flap or cover.

3.2.11   **Cold zone:** The area at a CBRN incident outside of the CBRN hazard area where the use of CBRN protective ensembles is not required because no CBRN hazard is present. (See 3.2.33, Hot Zone and 3.2.79, Warm Zone.)

3.2.12   **Compliant:** The condition of a CBRN protective ensemble model meeting or exceeding all applicable requirements of this standard, as determined pursuant and subject to *Law Enforcement CBRN Protective Ensemble Certification Program Requirements* (NIJ CR-0116.00).

3.2.13   **Component:** Any material, part or subassembly used in construction of the CBRN protective ensemble or ensemble element.[A]

3.2.14   **Composite:** Any layering of CBRN protective ensemble material(s), ensemble element materials or components as they appear in the final construction.[A]

3.2.15   **Duty belt:** A belt worn around the waist by law enforcement personnel to which essential equipment is attached.

3.2.16   **Duty uniform:** Non-CBRN protective ensemble apparel worn by law enforcement personnel on a regular basis during normal working conditions.

3.2.17   **Encapsulating ensemble:** A type of CBRN protective ensemble intended to provide protection to the upper and lower torso, head, hands and feet that completely covers the wearer and the wearer's respiratory protection.[A]

3.2.18   **Ensemble elements:** The four parts or items that compose CBRN protective ensembles including the garment, hand protection, foot protection and respiratory protection.

3.2.19   **Ensemble manufacturer:** Supplier of a CBRN protective ensemble who submits an ensemble model for certification.

3.2.20   **Flame impingement:** Direct contact between a flame and a material. (See ASTM Standard F1358, 3.13.)

3.2.21   **Flame resistance:** The property of a material whereby flaming combustion is prevented, terminated or inhibited following the application of a flaming or nonflaming source of ignition, with or without subsequent removal of the ignition source. [B]

3.2.22   **Flame-resistant (FR):** The quality of having flame resistance.

3.2.23   **Flame retardant:** A chemical used to impart flame resistance. (See ASTM Standard D123, 3.1.)

3.2.24   **Foot protection element:** An ensemble element intended to provide protection to the foot, ankle and lower leg from exposure to CBRN hazards.[A] There are three types of foot protection elements: (1) footwear, (2) footwear cover and (3) footwear liner. The CBRN protection may be in the form of a single type of foot protection element or a combination of types of foot protection elements.

3.2.25   **Foot protection upper:** The portion of a foot protection element above the sole.

3.2.26   **Footwear:** A type of foot protection element intended to cover and protect the foot, such as a boot or shoe.

3.2.27   **Footwear cover:** A type of foot protection element to be worn over footwear.

3.2.27.1   **Attached footwear cover:** A type of footwear cover similar to a boot that is constructed in such a manner as to be an extension of the garment leg.

3.2.27.2   **Detached footwear cover:** A type of footwear cover similar to a boot that is constructed in such a manner as to be separable from the garment and not an extension of the garment leg.

3.2.28   **Footwear liner:** A type of foot protection element that is sock-like, covers the entire foot and is intended to be worn inside footwear.

3.2.28.1   **Attached footwear liner:** A type of footwear liner constructed in such a manner as to be an extension of the garment leg.

3.2.28.2   **Detached footwear liner:** A type of footwear liner constructed in such a manner as to be separable from the garment and not an extension of the garment leg.

3.2.29   **Garment or garment element:** An ensemble element intended to provide protection to the upper and lower torso, arms, legs and head from exposure to CBRN hazards. There may be several types of garment element, such as an outer garment, a single-piece integrated garment or a multipiece integrated garment.

3.2.30   **Garment hardware:** Any parts of the garment that are not closures or the principal material, such as snaps, buttons and zipper pulls.

3.2.31   **Garment material:** Principal protective clothing material used in the construction of the garment element of the CBRN protective ensemble. This includes the visor material in garments utilizing visors.[A]

3.2.32   **Hand protection element:** A CBRN protective ensemble element intended to provide protection to the hands and wrists from exposure to CBRN hazards. There are two types of hand protection elements: (1) glove and (2) glove liner. The CBRN protection may be in the form of a single type of hand protection element or a combination of types of hand protection elements.

3.2.32.1   **Attached glove:** A type of glove constructed in such a manner as to be an extension of the garment sleeve.

3.2.32.2   **Attached glove liner:** A type of glove liner constructed in such a manner as to be an extension of the garment sleeve.

3.2.32.3   **Detached glove:** A type of glove constructed in such a manner as to be separable from the garment and not an extension of the garment sleeve.

3.2.32.4   **Detached glove liner:** A type of glove liner constructed in such a manner as to be separable from the garment and not an extension of the garment sleeve.

3.2.33   **Hot zone:** An area at a CBRN incident where CBRN hazards are present and the use of CBRN protective ensembles is required for purposes of safety. This area has the highest level of hazard. (See 3.2.79, Warm Zone and 3.2.10, Cold Zone.)

3.2.34   **Immediately dangerous to life and health (IDLH):** An atmospheric concentration of any toxic, corrosive or asphyxiant substance that poses an immediate threat to life or would interfere with an individual's ability to escape from a dangerous atmosphere. (See, e.g., 29 C.F.R. § 1910.120 (a)(3).)

3.2.35   **Interface:** (1) The meeting point between the garment element and a detached element of an ensemble, or (2) the mechanism intended to permit detached ensemble elements to be sealed to the garment element and to prevent unintentional separation of ensemble elements once sealed.

3.2.36   **Ionizing radiation:** Extremely high-energy radiation emitted from radioactive elements and isotopes.[A]

3.2.37   **Law enforcement response levels (LERLs):** Classification of CBRN protective ensembles based on mission requirements, expected mission duration, durability requirements of different operations and activities, and hazards in the CBRN threat environment. There are four LERLs: LERL-1, LERL-2, LERL-3 and LERL-4. (See 1.3.1.)

3.2.38   **Law enforcement specific equipment:** Equipment typically used by law enforcement personnel in performing their missions, including, but not limited to, weapons, restraining devices, communications equipment, body armor and ballistic helmets.

3.2.39   **Maintenance:** Inspection, repair and retirement of CBRN protective ensembles or ensemble elements.

3.2.40   **Man-in-simulant test (MIST):** A test to measure vapor leakage through chemical protective clothing ensembles, which involves a human subject wearing the ensemble inside a chamber filled with the vapor simulant MeS (methyl salicylate).

3.2.41   **Manufacturer:** A commercial enterprise engaged in fabricating a product.

3.2.42   **Methyl salicylate (MeS):** A chemical used as a simulant in the system level vapor protection test of this standard; also known as salicylic acid methyl ester, oil of wintergreen or betula oil.

3.2.43   **Mission duration:** The total time period for donning the CBRN protective ensemble, performing the assigned task(s) and doffing the CBRN protective ensemble.

3.2.44   **Model:** The manufacturer's design, with unique specifications and characteristics, of a particular item.

3.2.45 **Multipiece integrated garment:** A type of garment element that is designed and manufactured in such a manner so as to have more than one piece (such as a coat and pants).

3.2.46 **Multiple-use ensemble:** A CBRN protective ensemble intended to be worn more than once, but for only one exposure to a CBRN hazard. (See 3.2.66, Single-exposure ensemble and 3.2.68, Single-use ensemble.)

3.2.47 **Nonencapsulating ensemble:** A type of CBRN protective ensemble intended to provide whole body protection but that does not cover the wearer's respiratory protection.

3.2.48 **Outer garment:** A type of garment element that is worn over another type of garment element and that is required to satisfy this standard.[A]

3.2.49 **Passive absorbent dosimeters (PAD):** Adhesive-backed patches containing an absorbent material, which are placed on the skin at specific locations to collect any chemical vapor challenge that has infiltrated the protective ensemble. (See ASTM Standard F2588, 3.1.7.)

3.2.50 **Particulates:** Small particles of solid matter dispersed in air. There are at least seven forms of particulate matter, listed as follows[A]:

3.2.50.1 **Aerosol:** A dispersion of solid or liquid particles of microscopic size in a gaseous medium such as smoke, fog and mist.

3.2.50.2 **Dust:** Solid particles predominantly larger than colloidal and capable of temporary suspension in air or other gases.

3.2.50.3 **Fog:** Visible aerosols in which the dispersed phase is liquid, and formation by condensation is implied.

3.2.50.4 **Fume:** Solid particles generated at condensation from the gaseous state, generally after volatilization from melted substances and often accompanied by a chemical reaction, such as oxidation.

3.2.50.5 **Mist:** Dispersion of liquid particles, many of which are large enough to be individually visible without visual aid.

3.2.50.6 **Smog:** A term derived from the terms *smoke* and *fog* applied to extensive atmospheric contamination by aerosols arising from a combination of natural and man-made sources.

3.2.50.7 **Smoke:** Small gas-borne particles resulting from incomplete combustion and consisting predominantly of carbon and other combustible materials.

3.2.51 **Perimeter:** An established line defining a boundary between two areas or zones.

3.2.51.1 **Inner perimeter:** Defines the boundary between the hot zone and the warm zone. (See 3.2.33, Hot Zone and 3.2.789, Warm Zone.)

3.2.51.2   **Outer perimeter:** Defines the boundary between the warm zone and cold zone. (See 3.2.789, Warm Zone and 3.2.10, Cold Zone.)

3.2.52   **Perimeter operations:** Any operations requiring law enforcement personnel to conduct support tasks at perimeters (see 3.2.51, Perimeter), such as general security, access control and evacuation. These types of operations are typically conducted at the outer perimeter.

3.2.53   **Personal protective equipment:** Any item providing protection to the wearer against a hazard.

3.2.54   **Physical hazards:** A source of danger that may cause a breach of the CBRN protective ensemble or ensemble elements, such as abrasion wear, burst, cut, puncture, melting and seam separation.

3.2.55   **Physiological protective dosage factor (PPDF):** The factor by which protection is improved against effects from vapor exposure for the protected individual compared with whole body exposure of the unprotected individual. (See ASTM Standard F2588, 3.1.8.)

3.2.55.1   **Local PPDF ($PPDF_i$):** A PPDF at a specific location on the body. (See ASTM Standard F2588, 3.1.5.)

3.2.55.2   **Systemic PPDF ($PPDF_{sys}$):** A PPDF determined for an entire ensemble. (See ASTM Standard F2588, 3.1.10.)

3.2.56   **Product:** One unit of a particular model.

3.2.57   **Protective clothing material:** Material used in CBRN protective ensembles and ensemble elements for the purpose of protecting parts of the wearer's body against CBRN or physical hazards.[A]

3.2.58   **Radioactive particulates:** Small particles of radioactive materials dispersed in air, deposited on surfaces or deposited on or within a person. Radioactive particulates can be released to the environment through a nuclear power plant accident, the detonation of a nuclear device, an accidental release from a medical or industrial device, nuclear weapons testing or the intentional release of radioactive material through a criminal act or terrorism.

3.2.59   **Respiratory protection:** Equipment intended to cover at least the eyes, nose and mouth to protect the respiratory system and eyes from harmful particulates, vapors and gases.

3.2.59.1   **Air purifying respirator (APR):** A breathing apparatus with a filter that removes specific air contaminants by passing ambient air through the filter.

3.2.59.2   **Powered air purifying respirator (PAPR):** A positive pressure APR.

3.2.59.3   **Self-contained breathing apparatus (SCBA):** A type of respiratory protection in which the breathing air supply is carried by the user.

3.2.60   **Sample:** A CBRN protective ensemble, ensemble element, component or composite (or facsimile sample) that is to be subjected to conditioning procedures as specified in this standard in preparation for subsequent testing. A sample is to be representative of a model (or a model element, component or composite, as applicable).

3.2.60.1   **Facsimile sample:** A type of sample that is not taken from an actual CBRN protective ensemble, ensemble element, component or composite but that is prepared with materials and construction identical to an actual CBRN protective ensemble, ensemble element, component or composite.

3.2.61   **Seam:** Any permanent attachment of two or more materials, excluding external fittings, gaskets and garment closure assemblies, in a line formed by joining the separate material pieces.[A]

3.2.62   **Shall:** Indicates a mandatory requirement for the purposes of this voluntary standard.[A]

3.2.63   **Should:** Indicates a recommendation that is advised but not required for the purposes of this voluntary standard.[A]

3.2.64   **Shoulder weapon:** A rifle, shotgun or other type of long gun designed in such a manner so that the shooter rests the butt or the stock of the weapon against the shoulder and fires from shoulder level.

3.2.65   **Sight picture:** A visual image obtained by a shooter by viewing the intended target through the sighting system of a weapon.

3.2.66   **Single-exposure ensemble:** A CBRN protective ensemble intended to be worn multiple times, but for only one exposure to a CBRN hazard.

3.2.67   **Single-piece integrated garment:** A type of garment element that is designed and manufactured in such a manner so as to have only one piece (such as a one-piece coverall).

3.2.68   **Single-use ensemble:** A CBRN protective ensemble intended to be worn only one time, regardless of exposure to a CBRN hazard. (See 3.2.46, Multiple-use ensemble.)

3.2.69   **Specimen:** (1) A piece or portion of a sample to be tested (following conditioning as specified in this standard) that is representative of the whole sample, or (2) a complete sample to be tested (following conditioning as specified in this standard). (See 3.2.60, Sample.)

3.2.70   **Storage life:** The life expectancy of an unworn CBRN protective ensemble and its elements under ensemble manufacturer-recommended storage, care and maintenance conditions.

3.2.71   **Swatch:** Synonymous with *Specimen,* definition 1. (See 3.2.69, Specimen.)

3.2.72   **Tactical operations:** Law enforcement mission-specific tasks, such as an organized, armed response with the objective of conducting victim rescue or the mitigation of an immediate criminal human threat or hazard.

3.2.73   **Tactical uniform:** Non-CBRN apparel and equipment worn by tactical operations personnel.

3.2.74   **Tactical vest:** Ballistic body armor intended to protect against rifle fire. (See 3.2.22, Ballistic body armor)

3.2.75   **Toxic industrial chemical (TIC):** A highly toxic solid gaseous, liquid or solid substance that is routinely manufactured, stored, transported and used throughout the world.[1]

3.2.76   **Triethyl phosphate (TEP):** A chemical used as a simulant in the rain cabinet test of this standard.

3.2.77   **Visible breach of integrity:** An unintentional opening created in a CBRN protective ensemble during testing. The opening may be caused by failure of the material, such as, but not limited to, a rupture, puncture, tear or rip, failure of a closure or failure of an interface, such as, but not limited to, an interface between a hand protection element and sleeve, between a foot protection element and a garment leg or between a garment hood and respiratory protection.

3.2.78   **Visor:** Transparent component designed to protect the wearer's face and allow the wearer to see outside the CBRN protective ensemble.

3.2.79   **Warm zone:** The area at a CBRN incident between the hot zone and the cold zone where decontamination and hot zone support take place and where CBRN hazards are present to a lesser degree than in the hot zone. (See 3.2.9, Cold Zone and 3.2.33, Hot Zone.)

---

[1] See, e.g., OSHA "What are Toxic Industrial Chemicals?" at http://www.osha.gov/SLTC/emergencypreparedness/guides/chemical.html, April 17, 2007.

4. FORM AND FIT REQUIREMENTS

To be tested under the performance requirements of this standard, CBRN protective ensemble models must satisfy the requirements of this chapter.

4.1 Requirements for CBRN Protective Ensemble Models

4.1.1 CBRN protective ensembles shall meet or exceed the applicable requirements specified in this section.

4.1.2 CBRN protective ensembles shall be designed to protect the wearer's entire body including the head, upper and lower torso, arms, legs, hands and feet.[A]

4.1.3 CBRN protective ensembles may be designed for single use or multiple uses.

4.1.4 CBRN protective ensembles and ensemble elements may consist of a single layer or multiple layers.

4.1.5 CBRN protective ensembles may be either encapsulating or nonencapsulating.[A]

4.1.6 The integrated garment element of the CBRN protective ensemble may be either single-piece or multipiece.

4.1.7 CBRN protective ensembles shall accommodate the respiratory protection model(s) specified by the ensemble manufacturer for use with the specific ensemble model.[A]

4.1.8 All models of respiratory protection specified by the ensemble manufacturer for use with LERL-1, LERL-2, LERL-3 and LERL-4 CBRN protective ensembles shall be certified by NIOSH as approved to the performance requirements of *NIOSH Statement of Standard for CBRN SCBA, NIOSH Statement of Standard for CBRN APR* or *NIOSH Statement of Standard for CBRN PAPR.*[A] Respiratory protection that performs in multiple modes corresponding to various respiratory protection types, such as a combination SCBA/APR or combination SCBA/PAPR, must be certified by NIOSH as compliant in accordance with 42 C.F.R. Part 84. Each mode of operation and use of the respiratory protection with any of the LERL CBRN protective ensembles must comply with the applicable NIOSH CBRN respiratory protection approval criteria.

4.2 Requirements for Garment Element of CBRN Protective Ensemble Models

4.2.1 Garments shall meet or exceed the applicable requirements specified in this section.

4.2.2 Top-entry pockets shall have a cover flap with a closing mechanism.

4.2.3 Sewing thread utilized in the construction of LERL-1 garments shall be made of an inherently flame-resistant (FR) fiber.[C]

4.2.4 All garment hardware and closures shall be free of rough spots, burrs and sharp edges that could abrade or tear ensemble materials.[A]

4.2.5 Cargo pockets, where provided, shall have a means to drain water and shall have a means of being fastened in a closed position.[C]

4.2.6 Metallic closing mechanisms shall not come in direct contact with the body.[C]

4.2.7 Where garments and foot protection elements are integrated as a single piece, the foot protection elements shall be designed as an extension (attached) of the garment leg, so as to cover the entire lower leg, foot and ankle.[A]

4.2.8 Garments shall be made available in at least eight distinct sizes, which sizing shall be accomplished by the use of individual patterns for men's and women's garments.[A, C]

4.3 Requirements for Hand Protection Element of CBRN Protective Ensemble Models

4.3.1 Hand protection elements shall meet or exceed the applicable requirements specified in this section.

4.3.2 Hand protection elements shall provide protection from the fingertips to at least 25 mm (1 in) beyond the wrist crease.[A]

4.3.3 Gloves shall be made available in a minimum of five separate and distinct sizes ranging in hand length from 165 mm to 215 mm (6.4 in to 8.37 in) and in hand circumference from 165 mm to 245 mm (6.4 in to 9.55 in).[A] Hand length and circumference shall be measured as specified in Section 6.1 of EN 420, *Protective Gloves – General Requirements and Test Methods*, 2003.

4.3.4 Where glove liners are used as part of the ensemble, all glove liners shall accommodate glove sizes as referenced in Section 4.3.3.

4.4 Requirements for Foot Protection Element of CBRN Protective Ensemble Models

4.4.1 Foot protection elements shall meet or exceed the applicable requirements specified in this section.

4.4.2 Footwear, footwear liners and footwear covers shall provide protection of not less than 200 mm (8 in) in height when measured from the plane of the sole bottom.[A]

4.4.3 Where footwear liners are used as part of the CBRN protective ensemble, all footwear liners shall be made available in a minimum of eight distinct sizes ranging in length from 8.69 in (221 mm) in length to 12.31 in (313 mm).

4.4.4 Where footwear is used as part of the ensemble, it shall be made available in a minimum of eight distinct sizes ranging in length from 8.69 in (221 mm) in length to 12.31 in (313 mm).

4.4.5 Where footwear covers are used as part of the ensemble, all footwear covers shall accommodate footwear sizes as referenced in Section 4.4.4.

5.   PERFORMANCE REQUIREMENTS

5.1   LERL-1 CBRN Protective Ensemble Models

5.1.1   Ensemble (System Level) Model Requirements

5.1.1.1   LERL-1 ensembles shall be tested for entry of chemical vapor simulant as specified in Section 6.4, Man-In-Simulant Test (MIST), and shall have an average local physiological protective dosage factor ($PPDF_i$) value at each passive absorbent dosimeter (PAD) location for the four ensembles tested of no less than 360.0 and a systemic physiological protective dosage factor ($PPDF_{sys}$) value for each tested ensemble of no less than 361.0.[A]

5.1.1.2   Ergonomic Requirements[F,2]

5.1.1.2.1   LERL-1 ensembles shall be tested for donning time as specified in Section 6.6, Donning and Doffing Test, and shall have an average donning time for all elements of the LERL-1 ensemble of no greater than eight minutes. Ensembles shall not demonstrate any visible breach of integrity.

5.1.1.2.2   LERL-1 ensembles shall be tested for doffing time as specified in Section 6.6, Donning and Doffing Test, and shall have an average doffing time for all elements of the LERL-1 ensemble of no greater than three minutes. Ensembles shall not demonstrate any visible breach of integrity.

5.1.1.2.3   All gross body mobility tests referenced below shall be as specified in Section 6.7, Gross Body Mobility Tests.

5.1.1.2.4   LERL-1 ensembles shall not demonstrate any visible breach of integrity as a result of any of the tests specified in Section 6.7, Gross Body Mobility Tests.

5.1.1.2.5   LERL-1 ensembles shall be tested for gross body mobility as specified in Section 6.8, Forward Walking Test, and shall have an average percentage degradation in distance covered of less than 10%.

5.1.1.2.6   LERL-1 ensembles shall be tested for gross body mobility as specified in Section 6.9, Backward Walking Test, and shall have an average percentage degradation in distance covered of less than 10%.

5.1.1.2.7   LERL-1 ensembles shall be tested for gross body mobility as specified in Section 6.10, Side Step Walking Test, and shall have an average percentage degradation in distance covered of less than 10%.

---

[2] All subsections of 5.1.1.2 are derived from *Proposed Specifications for a Performance Standard for Chemical and Biological Protective Clothing and Equipment for Law Enforcement Operations* (see Table 5, Letter F of this document.)

5.1.1.2.8 LERL-1 ensembles shall be tested for gross body mobility as specified in Section 6.11, Upper Arm Abduction Test, and shall have an average percentage degradation in range of motion of less than 10%.

5.1.1.2.9 LERL-1 ensembles shall be tested for gross body mobility as specified in Section 6.12, Upper Arm Forward Extension Test, and shall have an average percentage degradation in range of motion of less than 10%.

5.1.1.2.10 LERL-1 ensembles shall be tested for gross body mobility as specified in Section 6.13, Upper Arm Backward Extension Test, and shall have an average percentage degradation in range of motion of less than 10%.

5.1.1.2.11 LERL-1 ensembles shall be tested for gross body mobility as specified in Section 6.14, Upper Leg Forward Extension Test, and shall have an average percentage degradation in range of motion of less than 10%.

5.1.1.2.12 LERL-1 ensembles shall be tested for gross body mobility as specified in Section 6.15, Upper Leg Backward Extension Test, and shall have an average percentage degradation in range of motion of less than 10%.

5.1.1.2.13 LERL-1 ensembles shall be tested for gross body mobility as specified in Section 6.16, Standing Trunk Flexion Test, and shall have an average percentage degradation in distance of less than 25%.

5.1.1.2.14 LERL-1 ensembles shall be tested for gross body mobility as specified in Section 6.17, Upper Leg Flexion Test, and shall have an average percent degradation in range of motion of less than 15%.

5.1.1.2.15 LERL-1 ensembles shall be tested for gross body mobility as specified in Section 6.18, Kneel and Rise Test, and the subject shall be able to rise from a kneeling position without assistance.

5.1.1.2.16 LERL-1 ensembles shall be tested for overall range of motion and functionality during a timed motion routine as specified in Section 6.19, Tactical Scenario Test, and shall have an average percent degradation in time of less than 20%. Completion of all specified tasks is required. Ensembles shall not demonstrate any visible breach of integrity.

5.1.1.2.17 LERL-1 hand protection elements shall be tested for gross hand dexterity as specified in Section 6.36, Glove Hand Function Test, and shall have overall percentage degradation over bare-handed manipulation of less than 35%. Ensembles shall not demonstrate any visible breach of integrity.

5.1.1.2.18 LERL-1 hand protection elements shall be tested for fine dexterity (hand manipulation) as specified in Section 6.37, Fine Finger Dexterity Test, and shall have an average percentage degradation over bare-handed manipulation of less than 50%. Ensembles shall not demonstrate any visible breach of integrity.

5.1.1.2.19 LERL-1 garments with the associated respiratory protection shall be tested as specified in Section 6.43, Field of View Test, and shall obtain a visual field score (VFS) of 90 or greater.

5.1.1.3 LERL-1 ensembles shall be tested for liquid penetration resistance as specified in Section 6.41, Overall Liquid Integrity Test, and shall show no liquid penetration following an eight-minute exposure.

5.1.1.4 LERL-1 ensembles shall be tested for audible signature as specified in Section 6.33, Audible Signature Test, and shall have an audible signature of 55 dBA or less.

5.1.2 **Garment Requirements for LERL-1 Ensemble Models**

5.1.2.1 LERL-1 garment materials and seams shall be tested for permeation resistance as specified in Section 6.22, Chemical Permeation Resistance Test, and shall meet the following performance criteria:[A]

- For permeation testing of the CWA Distilled sulfur mustard (HD), the cumulative permeation in one hour shall not exceed 4.0 $\mu g/cm^2$ for each specimen tested.

- For permeation testing of the CWA Soman (GD), the cumulative permeation in one hour shall not exceed 1.25 $\mu g/cm^2$ for each specimen tested.

- For permeation testing of liquid and gaseous TICs listed in Sections 6.22.3.3 and 6.22.3.4, the cumulative permeation in one hour shall not exceed 6.0 $\mu g/cm^2$ for each specimen tested.

5.1.2.2 LERL-1 garment materials and seams shall be tested for permeation resistance as specified in Section 6.23, LERL-1 Toxic Industrial Chemical Permeation Resistance Test, and shall meet the following performance criteria:

- For permeation testing of the liquid and gaseous TICs listed in Section 6.23, the breakthrough detection time shall be equal to or greater than one hour for each specimen tested calculated at a system detectable permeation rate of 0.10 $\mu g/cm^2/min.$[D]

5.1.2.3 LERL-1 garment materials and seams shall be tested for resistance to liquid or bloodborne pathogens as specified in Section 6.24, Viral Penetration Resistance Test, and shall allow no penetration of the Phi-X174 bacteriophage for one hour.[A]

5.1.2.4 LERL-1 garment material composites and seams shall be tested for resistance to liquid penetration under pressure as specified in Section 6.25, Expulsion Test, and shall allow no penetration for one hour using methyl salicylate (MeS).

5.1.2.5 LERL-1 garment material composites and seams shall be tested for resistance to liquid penetration when driven by rain as specified in Section 6.26, Rain Cabinet Test, and shall allow no penetration for one hour using triethyl phosphate (TEP) simulant.

5.1.2.6   LERL-1 woven garment materials shall be tested for tearing strength as specified in Section 6.27, Tearing Strength Test, and shall have a tear strength of not less than 50 N (11 lbf).[E]

5.1.2.7   LERL-1 garment materials shall be tested for cold weather performance as specified in Section 6.28, Cold Temperature Performance Test, and shall demonstrate no visible damage. [E]

5.1.2.8   LERL-1 nonwoven garment materials shall be tested for bursting strength as specified in Section 6.29, Burst Strength Test and shall have a bursting strength of not less than 350 N (79 lbf). [A, E]

5.1.2.9   LERL-1 garment seams/closures shall be tested for seam strength as specified in Section 6.30, Seam/Closure Breaking Strength Test, and shall have a breaking strength of not less than 500 N (112 lbf).[A]

5.1.2.10   LERL-1 garment composite materials shall be tested for cut resistance as specified in Section 6.31, Cut Resistance Test, and shall have a cut resistance blade travel of not less than 25 mm (1 in) with a weight of 200 grams (7 oz). [A, E]

5.1.2.11   LERL-1 garment composite materials shall be tested for puncture resistance as specified in Section 6.32, Puncture Resistance Test, and shall have a puncture resistance of not less than 10 N (2 lbf). [E]

5.1.2.12   LERL-1 garment composites shall be tested for total heat loss as specified in Section 6.34, Total Heat Loss Test, and shall have a total heat loss equal to or greater than 200 W/m^2 .[C]

5.1.2.13   LERL-1 garment textile fabrics intended to provide FR protection shall be individually tested for flame resistance as specified in Section 6.40, Flame Resistance Test, and shall not have a char length of more than 100 mm (4 in), shall not have an afterflame of more than two seconds and shall not melt or drip.[C, E]

5.1.2.14   LERL-1 zippers and seam-sealing materials shall meet the performance requirements specified in Section 5.1.2.13, where located on the exterior of the garment and not covered by the material intended to provide FR protection.[C]

5.1.2.15   LERL-1 garment composites shall be tested for thermal protective performance (TPP) as specified in Section 6.35, Thermal Protective Performance Test, and shall have an average TPP of eight or greater.[C, E]

5.1.2.16   LERL-1 garments shall be tested for flame protection as specified in Section 6.21, Flash Fire Test, and each specimen shall have a percentage of total body surface area (TBSA) of less than 25% (including 7% for the head).

5.1.2.17   LERL-1 garment outer materials shall be tested for color/visibility in accordance with Section 6.44, Color Visibility Test Method, and shall have a Y brightness value less than 25 and an L* value less than 55.

5.1.3 Hand Protection Element Requirements for LERL-1 Ensemble Models

5.1.3.1   Hand protection element types (gloves and glove liners) may be tested individually or in combination in order to meet the performance requirements outlined in this section.

- Where the hand protection element is composed of a single type of hand protection element, that element type shall meet all requirements of this section.

- Where the hand protection element is composed of multiple types of hand protection elements:
  - The outermost element type shall meet the requirements for cut resistance (Section 5.1.3.7), puncture resistance (Section 5.1.3.8), grip test (Section 5.1.3.10), FR (Section 5.1.4.114), TPP (Section 5.1.3.15) and color/visibility (Section 5.1.3.16).
  - The ensemble manufacturer shall indicate which of the element types is intended to meet the remaining requirements of this section.

5.1.3.2   LERL-1 hand protection element materials and seams shall be tested for permeation resistance as specified in Section 6.22, Chemical Permeation Resistance Test, and shall meet the following performance criteria:[A]

- For permeation testing of HD, the cumulative permeation in one hour shall not exceed 4.0 $\mu g/cm^2$ for each specimen tested.

- For permeation testing of GD, the cumulative permeation in one hour shall not exceed 1.25 $\mu g/cm^2$ for each specimen tested.

- For permeation testing of liquid and gaseous TICs listed in Sections 6.22.3.3 and 6.22.3.4, the cumulative permeation in one hour shall not exceed 6.0 $\mu g/cm^2$ for each specimen tested.

5.1.3.3   LERL-1 hand protection element materials and seams shall be tested for permeation resistance as specified in Section 6.23, LERL-1 Toxic Industrial Chemical Permeation Resistance Test, and shall meet the following performance criteria:

- For permeation testing of the liquid and gaseous TICs listed in Section 6.23, the breakthrough detection time shall be equal to or greater than one hour for each specimen tested calculated at a system detectable permeation rate of 0.10 $\mu g/cm^2/min.$[D]

5.1.3.4   LERL-1 hand protection element materials and seams shall be tested for resistance to liquid or bloodborne pathogens as specified in Section 6.24, Viral Penetration Resistance Test, and shall allow no penetration of the Phi-X174 bacteriophage for one hour.[A]

5.1.3.5   LERL-1 hand protection element material composites and seams shall be tested for resistance to liquid penetration under pressure as specified in Section 6.25, Expulsion Test, and shall allow no penetration for one hour using MeS.

5.1.3.6 LERL-1 hand protection element material composites and seams shall be tested for resistance to liquid penetration when driven by rain as specified in Section 6.26, Rain Cabinet Test, and shall allow no penetration for one hour using TEP simulant.

5.1.3.7 LERL-1 hand protection element composite materials shall be tested for cut resistance as specified in Section 6.31, Cut Resistance Test, and shall have a cut resistance blade travel of not less than 25 mm (1 in) with a weight of 200 grams (7 oz).[A]

5.1.3.8 LERL-1 hand protection element composite materials shall be tested for puncture resistance as specified in Section 6.32, Puncture Resistance Test, and shall have a puncture resistance of not less than 15 N (4 lbf).[A]

5.1.3.9 LERL-1 hand protection element materials shall be tested for cold weather performance as specified in Section 6.28, Cold Temperature Performance Test, and shall demonstrate no visible damage.

5.1.3.10 LERL-1 hand protection elements shall be tested for grip as specified in Section 6.38, Grip Test, and shall have a weight-pulling capacity not less than 95% of the bare-handed control values.

5.1.3.11 LERL-1 hand protection element seams shall be tested for seam strength as specified in Section 6.30, Seam/Closure Breaking Strength Test, and shall have a breaking strength of not less than 500 N (112 lbf).[A]

5.1.3.12 LERL-1 nonwoven hand protection element materials shall be tested for bursting strength as specified in Section 6.29, Burst Strength Test, and shall have a bursting strength of not less than 350 N (79 lbf). [A]

5.1.3.13 LERL-1 woven hand protection element materials shall be tested for tearing strength as specified in Section 6.27, Tearing Strength Test, and shall have a tear strength of not less than 50 N (11 lbf).

5.1.3.14 LERL-1 hand protection element textile fabrics intended to provide FR protection shall be individually tested for flame resistance as specified in Section 6.40, Flame Resistance Test, and shall not have a char length of more than 100 mm (4 in), shall not have an afterflame of more than two seconds and shall not melt or drip.[C]

5.1.3.15 LERL-1 hand protection element composites shall be tested for TPP as specified in Section 6.35, Thermal Protective Performance Test, and shall have an average TPP of eight or greater.[C]

5.1.3.16 LERL-1 hand protection element outer materials shall be tested for color/visibility in accordance with Section 6.44 and shall have a Y brightness value less than 25 and an L* value less than 55.

5.1.4   Foot Protection Element Requirements for LERL-1 Ensemble Models

5.1.4.1   Foot protection element types (footwear, footwear liners and footwear covers) may be tested individually or in combination in order to meet the performance requirements outlined in this section.

- Where the foot protection element is composed of a single type of foot protection element, that element type shall meet all requirements of this section.

- Where the foot protection element is composed of multiple types of foot protection elements:
    - The outermost element type shall meet the requirements for cut resistance (Section 5.1.4.7), puncture resistance (Section 5.1.4.8), abrasion resistance (Section 5.1.4.9), slip resistance (Section 5.1.4.10), FR (Section 5.1.4.11) and TPP (Section 5.1.4.12).
    - The ensemble manufacturer shall indicate which of the element types is intended to meet the remaining requirements of this section.

5.1.4.2   The appropriate LERL-1 foot protection element materials and seams shall be tested for permeation resistance as specified in Section 6.22, Chemical Permeation Resistance Test, and shall meet the following performance criteria:[A]

- For permeation testing of HD, the cumulative permeation in one hour shall not exceed 4.0 $\mu g/cm^2$ for each specimen tested.

- For permeation testing of GD, the cumulative permeation in one hour shall not exceed 1.25 $\mu g/cm^2$ for each specimen tested.

- For permeation testing of liquid and gaseous TICs listed in Sections 6.22.3.3 and 6.22.3.4, the cumulative permeation in one hour shall not exceed 6.0 $\mu g/cm^2$ for each specimen tested.

5.1.4.3   The appropriate LERL-1 foot protection element materials and seams shall be tested for permeation resistance as specified in Section 6.23, LERL-1 Toxic Industrial Chemical Permeation Resistance Test, and shall meet the following performance criteria:

- For permeation testing of the liquid and gaseous TICs listed in Section 6.23, the breakthrough detection time shall be equal to or greater than one hour for each specimen tested calculated at a system detectable permeation rate of 0.10 $\mu g/cm^2/min.$ [D]

5.1.4.4   The appropriate LERL-1 foot protection element materials and seams shall be tested for resistance to liquid or bloodborne pathogens as specified in Section 6.24, Viral Penetration Resistance Test, and shall allow no penetration of the Phi-X174 bacteriophage for one hour.[A]

5.1.4.5   The appropriate LERL-1 foot protection element materials and seams shall be tested for resistance to liquid penetration under pressure as specified in Section 6.25, Expulsion Test, and shall allow no penetration for one hour using MeS.

5.1.4.6   The appropriate LERL-1 foot protection element materials and seams shall be tested for resistance to liquid penetration when driven by rain as specified in Section 6.26, Rain Cabinet Test, and shall allow no penetration for one hour using TEP simulant.

5.1.4.7   The appropriate LERL-1 foot protection element materials shall be tested for cut resistance as specified in Section 6.31, Cut Resistance Test, and shall have a cut resistance blade travel of not less than 25 mm (1 in) with a weight of 200 grams (7 oz).[A]

5.1.4.8   The appropriate LERL-1 foot protection element materials shall be tested for puncture resistance as specified in Section 6.32, Puncture Resistance Test, and shall have a puncture resistance of not less than 36 N (8 lbf).[A]

5.1.4.9   The appropriate LERL-1 foot protection element soles and heels shall be tested for abrasion resistance as specified in Section 6.39, Abrasion Resistance Test, and have an abrasion resistance rating of not less than 65.[A]

5.1.4.10   The appropriate LERL-1 foot protection element soles and heels shall be tested for slip resistance as specified in Section 6.42, Slip Resistance Test, and shall have a static coefficient of 0.75 or greater.[A]

5.1.4.11   The appropriate LERL-1 foot protection element materials intended to provide FR protection shall be individually tested for FR as specified in Section 6.40, Flame Resistance Test, and shall not have a char length of more than 100 mm (4 in), shall not have an afterflame of more than two seconds and shall not melt or drip.[C]

5.1.4.12   The appropriate LERL-1 foot protection element fabric composites shall be tested for TPP as specified in Section 6.35, Thermal Protective Performance Test, and shall have an average TPP of eight or greater.[C]

5.1.4.13   The appropriate LERL-1 foot protection element outer materials shall be tested for color/visibility in accordance with Section 6.44, Color/Visibility Test Method, and shall have a Y brightness value less than 25 and an L* value less than 55.

5.2   LERL-2 CBRN Protective Ensemble Models

5.2.1   Ensemble (System Level) Model Requirements

5.2.1.1   LERL-2 ensembles shall be tested for entry of chemical vapor simulant as specified in Section 6.4, Man-In-Simulant Test (MIST), and shall have a $PPDF_i$ value at each PAD location for the four ensembles tested of no less than 360.0 and a $PPDF_{sys}$ value for each tested ensemble of no less than 361.0.[A]

5.2.1.2 Ergonomic Requirements[F,3]

5.2.1.2.1 LERL-2 ensembles shall be tested for donning time as specified in Section 6.6, Donning and Doffing Test, and shall have an average donning time for all elements of the LERL-2 ensemble of no greater than eight minutes. Ensembles shall not demonstrate any visible breach of integrity.

5.2.1.2.2 LERL-2 ensembles shall be tested for doffing time as specified in Section 6.6, Donning and Doffing Test, and shall have an average doffing time for all elements of the LERL-2 ensemble of no greater than three minutes. Ensembles shall not demonstrate any visible breach of integrity.

5.2.1.2.3 All gross body mobility tests referenced below shall be as specified in Section 6.7, Gross Body Mobility Tests.

5.2.1.2.4 LERL-2 ensembles shall not demonstrate any visible breach of integrity as a result of any of the tests specified in Section 6.7, Gross Body Mobility Tests.

5.2.1.2.5 LERL-2 ensembles shall be tested for gross body mobility as specified in Section 6.8, Forward Walking Test, and shall have an average percentage degradation in distance covered of less than 10%.

5.2.1.2.6 LERL-2 ensembles shall be tested for gross body mobility as specified in Section 6.9, Backward Walking Test, and shall have an average percentage degradation in distance covered of less than 10%.

5.2.1.2.7 LERL-2 ensembles shall be tested for gross body mobility as specified in Section 6.10, Side Step Walking Test, and shall have an average percentage degradation in distance covered of less than 10%.

5.2.1.2.8 LERL-2 ensembles shall be tested for gross body mobility as specified in Section 6.11, Upper Arm Abduction Test, and shall have an average percentage degradation in range of motion of less than 10%.

5.2.1.2.9 LERL-2 ensembles shall be tested for gross body mobility as specified in Section 6.12, Upper Arm Forward Extension Test, and shall have overall percentage degradation in range of motion of less than 10%.

5.2.1.2.10 LERL-2 ensembles shall be tested for gross body mobility as specified in Section 6.13, Upper Arm Backward Extension Test, and shall have an average percentage degradation in range of motion of less than 10%.

---

[3] All subsections of 5.2.1.2 are derived from *Proposed Specifications for a Performance Standard for Chemical and Biological Protective Clothing and Equipment for Law Enforcement Operations* (see Table 5, Letter F of this document.)

5.2.1.2.11 LERL-2 ensembles shall be tested for gross body mobility as specified in Section 6.14, Upper Leg Forward Extension Test, and shall have an average percentage degradation in range of motion of less than 10%.

5.2.1.2.12 LERL-2 ensembles shall be tested for gross body mobility as specified in Section 6.15, Upper Leg Backward Extension Test, and shall have an average percentage degradation in range of motion of less than 10%.

5.2.1.2.13 LERL-2 ensembles shall be tested for gross body mobility as specified in Section 6.16, Standing Trunk Flexion Test, and shall have an average percentage degradation in distance of less than 25%.

5.2.1.2.14 LERL-2 ensembles shall be tested for gross body mobility as specified in Section 6.17, Upper Leg Flexion Test, and shall have an average percent degradation in range of motion of less than 15%.

5.2.1.2.15 LERL-2 ensembles shall be tested for gross body mobility as specified in Section 6.18, Kneel and Rise Test, and the subject shall be able to rise from a kneeling position without assistance.

5.2.1.2.16 LERL-2 ensembles shall be tested for overall range of motion and functionality during a timed motion routine as specified in Section 6.19, Tactical Scenario Test, and shall have an average percent degradation in time of less than 20%. Completion of all specified tasks is required. Ensembles shall not demonstrate any visible breach of integrity.

5.2.1.2.17 LERL-2 hand protection elements shall be tested for hand function as specified in Section 6.36, Glove Hand Function Test, and shall have overall percentage degradation over bare-handed manipulation of less than 35%. Ensembles shall not demonstrate any visible breach of integrity.

5.2.1.2.18 LERL-2 hand protection elements shall be tested for fine dexterity (hand manipulation) as specified in Section 6.37, Fine Finger Dexterity Test, and shall have an average percentage degradation over bare-handed manipulation of less than 50%. Ensembles shall not demonstrate any visible breach of integrity.

5.2.1.2.19 LERL-2 garments with the associated respiratory protection shall be tested as specified in Section 6.43, Field of View Test, and shall obtain a VFS of 90 or greater.

5.2.1.3 LERL-2 ensembles shall be tested for liquid penetration resistance as specified in Section 6.41, Overall Liquid Integrity Test, and shall show no liquid penetration following an eight-minute exposure.

5.2.1.4 LERL-2 ensembles shall be tested for audible signature as specified in Section 6.33, Audible Signature Test, and shall have an audible signature of 55 dBA or less.

5.2.2   Garment Requirements for LERL-2 Ensemble Models

5.2.2.1   LERL-2 garment materials and seams shall be tested for permeation resistance as specified in Section 6.22, Chemical Permeation Resistance Test, and shall meet the following performance criteria:[A]

- For permeation testing of HD, the cumulative permeation in one hour shall not exceed 4.0 $\mu g/cm^2$ for each specimen tested.

- For permeation testing of GD, the cumulative permeation in one hour shall not exceed 1.25 $\mu g/cm^2$ for each specimen tested.

- For permeation testing of liquid and gaseous TICs, the cumulative permeation in one hour shall not exceed 6.0 $\mu g/cm^2$ for each specimen tested for the chemicals listed in Sections 6.22.3.3 and 6.22.3.4.

5.2.2.2   LERL-2 garment materials and seams shall be tested for resistance to liquid or bloodborne pathogens as specified in Section 6.24, Viral Penetration Resistance Test, and shall allow no penetration of the Phi-X174 bacteriophage for one hour.[A]

5.2.2.3   LERL-2 garment material composites and seams shall be tested for resistance to liquid penetration under pressure as specified in Section 6.25, Expulsion Test, and shall allow no penetration for one hour using MeS.

5.2.2.4   LERL-2 garment material composites and seams shall be tested for resistance to liquid penetration when driven by rain as specified in Section 6.26, Rain Cabinet Test, and shall allow no penetration for one hour using TEP simulant.

5.2.2.5   LERL-2 woven garment materials shall be tested for tearing strength as specified in Section 6.27, Tearing Strength Test, and shall have a tear strength of not less than 50 N (11 lbf). [E]

5.2.2.6   LERL-2 garment materials shall be tested for cold weather performance as specified in Section 6.28, Cold Temperature Performance Test, and shall demonstrate no visible damage. [E]

5.2.2.7   LERL-2 nonwoven garment materials shall be tested for bursting strength as specified in Section 6.29, Burst Strength Test, and shall have a bursting strength of not less than 350 N (79 lbf). [E]

5.2.2.8   LERL-2 garment seams/closures shall be tested for seam strength as specified in Section 6.30, Seam/Closure Breaking Strength Test, and shall have a breaking strength of not less than 500 N (112 lbf).[A]

5.2.2.9   LERL-2 garment composite materials shall be tested for cut resistance as specified in Section 6.31, Cut Resistance Test, and shall have a cut resistance blade travel of not less than 25 mm (1 in) with a weight of 200 grams (7 oz). [E, A]

5.2.2.10 LERL-2 garment composite materials shall be tested for puncture resistance as specified in Section 6.32, Puncture Resistance Test, and shall have a puncture resistance of not less than 10 N (2 lbf). [E]

5.2.2.11 LERL-2 garment composites shall be tested for total heat loss as specified in Section 6.34, Total Heat Loss Test and shall have a total heat loss equal to or greater than 250 W/m^2. [C]

5.2.2.12 LERL-2 garment composites shall be tested for flammability as specified in Section 6.5, Flame Impingement Test, and shall demonstrate no afterflame, no melt and no drip after the initial three-second exposure.

5.2.2.13 LERL-2 garment outer materials shall be tested for color/visibility in accordance with Section 6.44, Color/Visibility Test, and shall have a Y brightness value less than 25 and an L* value less than 55.

5.2.3 **Hand Protection Element Requirements for LERL-2 Ensemble Models**

5.2.3.1 Hand protection element types (gloves and glove liners) may be tested individually or in combination in order to meet the performance requirements outlined in this section.

- Where the hand protection element is composed of a single type of hand protection element, that element type shall meet all requirements of this section.

- Where the hand protection element is composed of multiple types of hand protection elements:
  - The outermost element type shall meet the requirements for cut resistance (Section 5.2.3.6), puncture resistance (Section 5.2.3.7), grip test (Section 5.2.3.9), flammability (Section 5.2.3.13) and color/visibility (Section 5.2.3.14).
  - The ensemble manufacturer shall indicate which of the element types is intended to meet the remaining requirements of this section.

5.2.3.2 LERL-2 hand protection element materials and seams shall be tested for permeation resistance as specified in Section 6.22, Chemical Permeation Resistance Test, and shall meet the following performance criteria:[A]

- For permeation testing of HD, the cumulative permeation in one hour shall not exceed 4.0 $\mu g/cm^2$ for each specimen tested.

- For permeation testing of GD, the average permeation in one hour shall not exceed 1.25 $\mu g/cm^2$ for each specimen tested.

- For permeation testing of liquid and gaseous TICs, the cumulative permeation in one hour shall not exceed 6.0 $\mu g/cm^2$ for each specimen tested for the chemicals listed in Sections 6.22.3.3 and 6.22.3.4.

5.2.3.3 LERL-2 hand protection element materials and seams shall be tested for resistance to liquid or bloodborne pathogens as specified in Section 6.24, Viral Penetration

Resistance Test, and shall allow no penetration of the Phi-X174 bacteriophage for one hour.[A]

5.2.3.4 LERL-2 hand protection element material composites and seams shall be tested for resistance to liquid penetration under pressure as specified in Section 6.25, Expulsion Test, and shall allow no penetration for one hour using MeS.

5.2.3.5 LERL-2 hand protection element material composites and seams shall be tested for resistance to liquid penetration when driven by rain as specified in Section 6.26, Rain Cabinet Test, and shall allow no penetration for one hour using TEP simulant.

5.2.3.6 LERL-2 hand protection element composite materials shall be tested for cut resistance as specified in Section 6.31, Cut Resistance Test, and shall have a cut resistance blade travel of not less than 25 mm (1 in) with a weight of 200 grams (7 oz).[A]

5.2.3.7 LERL-2 hand protection element composite materials shall be tested for puncture resistance as specified in Section 6.32, Puncture Resistance Test, and shall have a puncture resistance of not less than 15 N (4 lbf).[A]

5.2.3.8 LERL-2 hand protection element materials shall be tested for cold weather performance as specified in Section 6.28, Cold Temperature Performance Test, and shall demonstrate no visible damage.

5.2.3.9 LERL-2 hand protection elements shall be tested for grip as specified in Section 6.38, Grip Test, and shall have a weight-pulling capacity not less than 95% of the bare-handed control values.

5.2.3.10 LERL-2 hand protection element seams shall be tested for seam strength as specified in Section 6.30, Seam/Closure Breaking Strength Test, and shall have a breaking strength of not less than 500 N (112 lbf). [A]

5.2.3.11 LERL-2 nonwoven hand protection element materials shall be tested for bursting strength as specified in Section 6.29, Burst Strength Test, and shall have a bursting strength of not less than 350 N (79 lbf). [A]

5.2.3.12 LERL-2 woven hand protection element materials shall be tested for tearing strength as specified in Section 6.27, Tearing Strength Test, and shall have a tear strength of not less than 50 N (11 lbf).

5.2.3.13 LERL-2 hand protection element composites shall be tested for flammability as specified in Section 6.5, Flame Impingement Test, and shall demonstrate no afterflame, no melt and no drip after the initial three-second exposure.

5.2.3.14 LERL-2 hand protection element outer materials shall be tested for color/visibility in accordance with Section 6.44, Color/Visibility Test Method, and shall have a Y brightness value less than 25 and an L* value less than 55.

5.2.4   Foot Protection Element Requirements for LERL-2 Ensemble Models

5.2.4.1   Foot protection element types (footwear, footwear liners and footwear covers) may be tested individually or in combination in order to meet the performance requirements outlined in this section.

- Where the foot protection element is composed of a single type of foot protection element, that element type shall meet all requirements of this section.

- Where the foot protection element is composed of multiple types of foot protection elements:
  o The outermost element type shall meet the requirements for cut resistance (Section 5.2.4.6), puncture resistance (Section 5.2.4.7), abrasion resistance (Section 5.2.4.8), slip resistance (Section 5.2.4.9) and flammability (Section 5.2.4.10).
  o The ensemble manufacturer shall indicate which of the element types is intended to meet the remaining requirements of this section.

5.2.4.2   The appropriate LERL-2 foot protection element materials and seams shall be tested for permeation resistance as specified in Section 6.22, Chemical Permeation Resistance Test, and shall meet the following performance criteria:[A]

- For permeation testing of HD, the cumulative permeation in one hour shall not exceed 4.0 $\mu g/cm^2$ for each specimen tested.

- For permeation testing of GD, the cumulative permeation in one hour shall not exceed 1.25 $\mu g/cm^2$ for each specimen tested.

- For permeation testing of liquid and gaseous TICs listed in Sections 6.22.3.3 and 6.22.3.4, the cumulative permeation in one hour shall not exceed 6.0 $\mu g/cm^2$ for each specimen tested.

5.2.4.3   The appropriate LERL-2 foot protection element materials and seams shall be tested for resistance to liquid or bloodborne pathogens as specified in Section 6.24, Viral Penetration Resistance Test, and shall allow no penetration of the Phi-X174 bacteriophage for one hour.[A]

5.2.4.4   The appropriate LERL-2 foot protection element materials and seams shall be tested for resistance to liquid penetration under pressure as specified in Section 6.25, Expulsion Test, and shall allow no penetration for one hour using MeS.

5.2.4.5   The appropriate LERL-2 foot protection element materials and seams shall be tested for resistance to liquid penetration when driven by rain as specified in Section 6.26, Rain Cabinet Test, and shall allow no penetration for one hour using TEP simulant.

5.2.4.6   The appropriate LERL-2 foot protection element materials shall be tested for cut resistance as specified in Section 6.31, Cut Resistance Test, and shall have a cut resistance blade travel of not less than 25 mm (1 in) with a weight of 200 grams (7 oz).[A]

5.2.4.7 The appropriate LERL-2 foot protection element materials shall be tested for puncture resistance as specified in Section 6.32, Puncture Resistance Test, and shall have a puncture resistance of not less than 36 N (8 lbf).[A]

5.2.4.8 The appropriate LERL-2 foot protection element soles and heels shall be tested for abrasion resistance as specified in Section 6.39, Abrasion Resistance Test, and have an abrasion resistance rating of not less than 65.[A]

5.2.4.9 The appropriate LERL-2 foot protection element soles and heels shall be tested for slip resistance as specified in Section 6.42, Slip Resistance Test, and shall have a static coefficient of 0.75 or greater.[A]

5.2.4.10 The appropriate LERL-2 foot protection element materials shall be tested for flammability as specified in Section 6.5, Flame Impingement Test, and shall demonstrate no afterflame, no melt and no drip after the initial three-second exposure.

5.2.4.11 The appropriate LERL-2 foot protection element outer materials shall be tested for color/visibility in accordance with Section 6.44, Color/Visibility Test Method, and shall have a Y brightness value less than 25 and an L* value less than 55.

5.3 LERL-3 CBRN Protective Ensemble Models

5.3.1 Ensemble (System Level) Model Requirements

5.3.1.1 LERL-3 ensembles shall be tested for entry of chemical vapor simulant as specified in Section 6.4, Man-In-Simulant Test (MIST), and shall have a $PPDF_i$ value at each PAD location for the four ensembles tested of no less than 120.0 and a $PPDF_{sys}$ value for each tested ensemble of no less than 76.0.[A]

5.3.1.2 Ergonomic Requirements[F,4]

5.3.1.2.1 LERL-3 ensembles shall be tested for donning time as specified in Section 6.6, Donning and Doffing Test, and shall have an average donning time for all elements of the LERL-3 ensemble of no greater than seven minutes. Ensembles shall not demonstrate any visible breach of integrity.

5.3.1.2.2 LERL-3 ensembles shall be tested for doffing time as specified in Section 6.6, Donning and Doffing Test, and shall have an average doffing time for all elements of the LERL-3 ensemble of no greater than three minutes. Ensembles shall not demonstrate any visible breach of integrity.

---

[4] All subsections of 5.3.1.2 are derived from *Proposed Specifications for a Performance Standard for Chemical and Biological Protective Clothing and Equipment for Law Enforcement Operations* (see Table 5, Letter F of this document.)

5.3.1.2.3 All gross body mobility tests referenced below shall be as specified in Section 6.7, Gross Body Mobility Tests.

5.3.1.2.4 LERL-3 ensembles shall not demonstrate any visible breach of integrity as a result of any of the tests specified in Section 6.7, Gross Body Mobility Tests.

5.3.1.2.5 LERL-3 ensembles shall be tested for gross body mobility as specified in Section 6.8, Forward Walking Test, and shall have an average percentage degradation in distance covered of less than 10%.

5.3.1.2.6 LERL-3 ensembles shall be tested for gross body mobility as specified in Section 6.9, Backward Walking Test, and shall have an average percentage degradation in distance covered of less than 10%.

5.3.1.2.7 LERL-3 ensembles shall be tested for gross body mobility as specified in Section 6.10, Side Step Walking Test, and shall have an average percentage degradation in distance covered of less than 10%.

5.3.1.2.8 LERL-3 ensembles shall be tested for gross body mobility as specified in Section 6.11, Upper Arm Abduction Test, and shall have an average percentage degradation in range of motion of less than 10%.

5.3.1.2.9 LERL-3 ensembles shall be tested for gross body mobility as specified in Section 6.12, Upper Arm Forward Extension Test, and shall have an average percentage degradation in range of motion of less than 10%.

5.3.1.2.10 LERL-3 ensembles shall be tested for gross body mobility as specified in Section 6.13, Upper Arm Backward Extension Test, and shall have an average percentage degradation in range of motion of less than 10%.

5.3.1.2.11 LERL-3 ensembles shall be tested for gross body mobility as specified in Section 6.14, Upper Leg Forward Extension Test, and shall have an average percentage degradation in range of motion of less than 10%.

5.3.1.2.12 LERL-3 ensembles shall be tested for gross body mobility as specified in Section 6.15, Upper Leg Backward Extension Test, and shall have an average percentage degradation in range of motion of less than 10%.

5.3.1.2.13 LERL-3 ensembles shall be tested for gross body mobility as specified in Section 6.16, Standing Trunk Flexion Test, and shall have an average percentage degradation in distance of less than 25%.

5.3.1.2.14 LERL-3 ensembles shall be tested for gross body mobility as specified in Section 6.17, Upper Leg Flexion Test, and shall have an average percent degradation in range of motion of less than 15%.

5.3.1.2.15 LERL-3 ensembles shall be tested for gross body mobility as specified in Section 6.18, Kneel and Rise Test, and the subject shall be able to rise from a kneeling position without assistance.

5.3.1.2.16 LERL-3 ensembles shall be tested for overall range of motion and functionality during a timed motion routine as specified in Section 6.19, Tactical Scenario Test, and shall have an average percent degradation in time of less than 20%. Completion of all specified tasks is required. Ensembles shall not demonstrate any visible breach of integrity.

5.3.1.2.17 LERL-3 hand protection elements shall be tested for hand function as specified in Section 6.36, Glove Hand Function Test, and shall have overall percentage degradation over bare-handed manipulation of less than 35%. Ensembles shall not demonstrate any visible breach of integrity.

5.3.1.2.18 LERL-3 hand protection elements shall be tested for fine dexterity (hand manipulation) as specified in Section 6.37, Fine Finger Dexterity Test, and shall have an average percentage degradation over bare-handed manipulation of less than 50%. Ensembles shall not demonstrate any visible breach of integrity.

5.3.1.2.19 LERL-3 garments with the associated respiratory protection shall be tested as specified in Section 6.43, Field of View Test, and shall obtain a VFS of 90 or greater.

5.3.1.3 The LERL-3 ensembles shall be tested for liquid penetration resistance as specified in Section 6.41, Overall Liquid Integrity Test, and shall show no liquid penetration following a four-minute exposure.

5.3.1.4 LERL-3 ensembles shall be tested for audible signature as specified in Section 6.33, Audible Signature Test, and shall have an audible signature of 45 dBA or less.

5.3.2 **Garment Requirements for LERL-3 Ensemble Models**

5.3.2.1 LERL-3 garment materials and seams shall be tested for permeation resistance as specified in Section 6.22, Chemical Permeation Resistance Test, and shall meet the following performance criteria:[A]

- For permeation testing of HD, the cumulative permeation in one hour shall not exceed 4.0 $\mu g /cm^2$ for each specimen tested.

- For permeation testing of GD, the cumulative permeation in one hour shall not exceed 1.25 $\mu g /cm^2$ for each specimen tested.

- For permeation testing of liquid and gaseous TICs, the cumulative permeation in one hour shall not exceed 6.0 $\mu g /cm^2$ for each specimen tested for the chemicals listed in Sections 6.22.3.3 and 6.22.3.4.

5.3.2.2 LERL-3 garment materials and seams shall be tested for resistance to liquid or bloodborne pathogens as specified in Section 6.24, Viral Penetration Resistance Test, and shall allow no penetration of the Phi-X174 bacteriophage for one hour.[A]

5.3.2.3 LERL-3 garment material composites and seams shall be tested for resistance to liquid penetration under pressure as specified in Section 6.25, Expulsion Test, and shall allow no penetration for one hour using MeS.

5.3.2.4 LERL-3 garment material composites and seams shall be tested for resistance to liquid penetration when driven by rain as specified in Section 6.26, Rain Cabinet Test, and shall allow no penetration for one hour using TEP simulant.

5.3.2.5 LERL-3 woven garment materials shall be tested for tearing strength as specified in Section 6.27, Tearing Strength Test, and shall have a tear strength of not less than 50 N (11 lbf).[E]

5.3.2.6 LERL-3 garment materials shall be tested for cold weather performance as specified in Section 6.28, Cold Temperature Performance Test, and shall demonstrate no visible damage.[E]

5.3.2.7 LERL-3 nonwoven garment materials shall be tested for bursting strength as specified in Section 6.29, Burst Strength Test, and shall have a bursting strength of not less than 350 N (79 lbf).[A, E]

5.3.2.8 LERL-3 garment seams/closures shall be tested for seam strength as specified in Section 6.30, Seam/Closure Breaking Strength Test, and shall have a breaking strength of not less than 500 N (112 lbf).[A]

5.3.2.9 LERL-3 garment materials shall be tested for cut resistance as specified in Section 6.31, Cut Resistance Test, and shall have a cut resistance blade travel of not less than 25 mm (1 in) with a weight of 200 grams (7 oz).[A, E]

5.3.2.10 LERL-3 garment materials shall be tested for puncture resistance as specified in Section 6.32, Puncture Resistance Test, and shall have a puncture resistance of not less than 10 N (2 lbf).[E]

5.3.2.11 LERL-3 garment composites shall be tested for total heat loss as specified in Section 6.34, Total Heat Loss Test, and shall have a total heat loss equal to or greater than 450 W/m^2.[C]

5.3.2.12 LERL-3 garment composites shall be tested for flammability as specified in Section 6.5, Flame Impingement Test, and shall demonstrate no afterflame, no melt and no drip after the initial three-second exposure.

5.3.2.13 LERL-3 garment outer materials shall be tested for color/visibility in accordance with Section 6.44, Color/Visibility Test Method, and shall have a Y brightness value less than 25 and an L* value less than 55.

5.3.3 **Hand Protection Element Requirements for LERL-3 Ensemble Models**

5.3.3.1 Hand protection element types (gloves and glove liners) may be tested individually or in combination in order to meet the performance requirements outlined in this section.

- Where the hand protection element is composed of a single type of hand protection element, that element type shall meet all requirements of this section.

- Where the hand protection element is composed of multiple types of hand protection elements:
    - The outermost element type shall meet the requirements for cut resistance (Section 5.3.3.6), puncture resistance (Section 5.3.3.7), grip test (Section 5.3.3.9), flammability (Section 5.3.3.13) and color/visibility (Section 5.3.3.14).
    - The ensemble manufacturer shall indicate which of the element types is intended to meet the remaining requirements of this section.

5.3.3.2 LERL-3 hand protection element materials and seams shall be tested for permeation resistance as specified in Section 6.22, Chemical Permeation Resistance Test, and shall meet the following performance criteria:[A]

- For permeation testing of HD, the cumulative permeation in one hour shall not exceed 4.0 µg/cm^2 for each specimen tested.

- For permeation testing of GD, the cumulative permeation in one hour shall not exceed 1.25 µg/cm^2 for each specimen tested.

- For permeation testing of liquid and gaseous TICs, the cumulative permeation in one hour shall not exceed 6.0 µg/cm^2 for each specimen tested for the chemicals listed in Sections 6.22.3.3 and 6.22.3.4.

5.3.3.3 LERL-3 hand protection element materials and seams shall be tested for resistance to liquid or bloodborne pathogens as specified in Section 6.24, Viral Penetration Resistance Test, and shall allow no penetration of the Phi-X174 bacteriophage for one hour.[A]

5.3.3.4 LERL-3 hand protection element material composites and seams shall be tested for resistance to liquid penetration under pressure as specified in Section 6.25, Expulsion Test, and shall allow no penetration for one hour using MeS.

5.3.3.5 LERL-3 hand protection element material composites and seams shall be tested for resistance to liquid penetration when driven by rain as specified in Section 6.26, Rain Cabinet Test, and shall allow no penetration for one hour using TEP simulant.

5.3.3.6 LERL-3 hand protection element materials shall be tested for cut resistance as specified in Section 6.31, Cut Resistance Test, and shall have a cut resistance blade travel of not less than 25 mm (1 in) with a weight of 200 grams (7 oz).[A]

5.3.3.7 LERL-3 hand protection element materials shall be tested for puncture resistance as specified in Section 6.32, Puncture Resistance Test, and shall have a puncture resistance of not less than 15 N (4 lbf).[A]

5.3.3.8 LERL-3 hand protection element materials shall be tested for cold weather performance as specified in Section 6.28, Cold Temperature Performance Test, and shall demonstrate no visible damage.

5.3.3.9 LERL-3 hand protection elements shall be tested for grip as specified in Section 6.38, Grip Test, and shall have a weight-pulling capacity not less than 95% of the bare-handed control values.

5.3.3.10 LERL-3 hand protection element seams shall be tested for seam strength as specified in Section 6.30, Seam/Closure Breaking Strength Test, and shall have a breaking strength of not less than 500 N (112 lbf).[A]

5.3.3.11 LERL-3 nonwoven hand protection element materials shall be tested for bursting strength as specified in Section 6.29, Burst Strength Test, and shall have a bursting strength of not less than 350 N (79 lbf).[A]

5.3.3.12 LERL-3 woven hand protection element materials shall be tested for tearing strength as specified in Section 6.27, Tearing Strength Test, and shall have a tear strength of not less than 50 N (11 lbf).

5.3.3.13 LERL-3 hand protection element composites shall be tested for flammability as specified in Section 6.5, Flame Impingement Test, and shall demonstrate no afterflame, no melt and no drip after the initial three-second exposure.

5.3.3.14 LERL-3 hand protection element outer materials shall be tested for color/visibility in accordance with Section 6.44, Color/Visibility Test Method, and shall have a Y brightness value less than 25 and an L* value less than 55.

5.3.4 Foot Protection Element Requirements for LERL-3 Ensemble Models

5.3.4.1 Foot protection element types (footwear, footwear liners and footwear covers) may be tested individually or in combination in order to meet the performance requirements outlined in this section.

- Where the foot protection element is composed of a single type of foot protection element, that element type shall meet all requirements of this section.

- Where the foot protection element is composed of multiple types of foot protection elements:
    - The outermost element type shall meet the requirements for cut resistance (Section 5.3.4.6), puncture resistance (Section 5.3.4.7), abrasion resistance (Section 5.3.4.8), slip resistance (Section 5.3.4.9) and flammability (Section 5.3.4.10).

o   The ensemble manufacturer shall indicate which of the element types is intended to meet the remaining requirements of this section.

5.3.4.2   The appropriate LERL-3 foot protection element materials and seams shall be tested for permeation resistance as specified in Section 6.22, Chemical Permeation Resistance Test, and shall meet the following performance criteria:[A]

- For permeation testing of HD, the cumulative permeation in one hour shall not exceed 4.0 $\mu g/cm^2$ for each specimen tested.

- For permeation testing of GD, the cumulative permeation in one hour shall not exceed 1.25 $\mu g/cm^2$ for each specimen tested.

- For permeation testing of liquid and gaseous TICs listed in Sections 6.22.3.3 and 6.22.3.4, the cumulative permeation in one hour shall not exceed 6.0 $\mu g/cm^2$ for each specimen tested.

5.3.4.3   The appropriate LERL-3 foot protection element materials and seams shall be tested for resistance to liquid or bloodborne pathogens as specified in Section 6.24, Viral Penetration Resistance Test, and shall allow no penetration of the Phi-X174 bacteriophage for one hour.[A]

5.3.4.4   The appropriate LERL-3 foot protection element materials and seams shall be tested for resistance to liquid penetration under pressure as specified in Section 6.25, Expulsion Test, and shall allow no penetration for one hour using MeS.

5.3.4.5   The appropriate LERL-3 foot protection element materials and seams shall be tested for resistance to liquid penetration when driven by rain as specified in Section 6.26, Rain Cabinet Test, and shall allow no penetration for one hour using TEP simulant.

5.3.4.6   The appropriate LERL-3 foot protection element materials shall be tested for cut resistance as specified in Section 6.31, Cut Resistance Test, and shall have a cut resistance blade travel of not less than 25 mm (1 in) with a weight of 200 grams (7 oz).[A]

5.3.4.7   The appropriate LERL-3 foot protection element materials shall be tested for puncture resistance as specified in Section 6.32, Puncture Resistance Test, and shall have a puncture resistance of not less than 36 N (8 lbf).[A]

5.3.4.8   The appropriate LERL-3 foot protection element soles and heels shall be tested for abrasion resistance as specified in Section 6.39, Abrasion Resistance Test, and have an abrasion resistance rating of not less than 65.[A]

5.3.4.9   The appropriate LERL-3 foot protection element soles and heels shall be tested for slip resistance as specified in Section 6.42, Slip Resistance Test, and shall have a static coefficient of 0.75 or greater.[A]

5.3.4.10 The appropriate LERL-3 foot protection element materials shall be tested for flammability as specified in Section 6.5, Flame Impingement Test, and shall demonstrate no afterflame, no melt and no drip after the initial three-second exposure.

5.3.4.11 The appropriate LERL-3 foot protection element outer materials shall be tested for color/visibility in accordance with Section 6.44, Color/Visibility Test Method, and shall have a Y brightness value less than 25 and an L* value less than 55.

5.4   LERL-4 CBRN Protective Ensemble Models

5.4.1   Ensemble (System Level) Model Requirements

5.4.1.1 LERL-4 ensembles shall be tested for overall inward leakage as specified in Section 6.4, Man-In-Simulant Test (MIST), and shall have a $PPDF_i$ value at each PAD location for the four ensembles tested of no less than 120.0 and a $PPDF_{sys}$ value for each tested ensemble of no less than 76.0.[A]

5.4.1.2   Ergonomic Requirements[F,5]

5.4.1.2.1 LERL-4 ensembles shall be tested for donning time as specified in Section 6.6, Donning and Doffing Test, and shall have an average donning time for all elements of the LERL-4 ensemble of no greater than seven minutes. Ensembles shall not demonstrate any visible breach of integrity.

5.4.1.2.2 LERL-4 ensembles shall be tested for doffing time as specified in Section 6.6, Donning and Doffing Test, and shall have an average doffing time for all elements of the LERL-4 ensemble of no greater than three minutes. Ensembles shall not demonstrate any visible breach of integrity.

5.4.1.2.3 All gross body mobility tests referenced below shall be as specified in Section 6.7, Gross Body Mobility Tests.

5.4.1.2.4 LERL-4 ensembles shall not demonstrate any visible breach of integrity as a result of any of the tests specified in Section 6.7, Gross Body Mobility Tests.

5.4.1.2.5 LERL-4 ensembles shall be tested for gross body mobility as specified in Section 6.8, Forward Walking Test, and shall have an average percentage degradation in distance covered of less than 10%.

5.4.1.2.6 LERL-4 ensembles shall be tested for gross body mobility as specified in Section 6.9, Backward Walking Test, and shall have an average percentage degradation in distance covered of less than 10%.

---

[5] All subsections of 5.4.1.2 are derived from *Proposed Specifications for a Performance Standard for Chemical and Biological Protective Clothing and Equipment for Law Enforcement Operations* (see Table 5, Letter F of this document.)

5.4.1.2.7 LERL-4 ensembles shall be tested for gross body mobility as specified in Section 6.10, Side Step Walking Test, and shall have an average percentage degradation in distance covered of less than 10%.

5.4.1.2.8 LERL-4 ensembles shall be tested for gross body mobility as specified in Section 6.11, Upper Arm Abduction Test, and shall have an average percentage degradation in range of motion of less than 10%.

5.4.1.2.9 LERL-4 ensembles shall be tested for gross body mobility as specified in Section 6.12, Upper Arm Forward Extension Test, and shall have an average percentage degradation in range of motion of less than 10%.

5.4.1.2.10 LERL-4 ensembles shall be tested for gross body mobility as specified in Section 6.13, Upper Arm Backward Extension Test, and shall have an average percentage degradation in range of motion of less than 10%.

5.4.1.2.11 LERL-4 ensembles shall be tested for gross body mobility as specified in Section 6.14, Upper Leg Forward Extension Test, and shall have an average percentage degradation in range of motion of less than 10%.

5.4.1.2.12 LERL-4 ensembles shall be tested for gross body mobility as specified in Section 6.15, Upper Leg Backward Extension Test, and shall have an average percentage degradation in range of motion of less than 10%.

5.4.1.2.13 LERL-4 ensembles shall be tested for gross body mobility as specified in Section 6.16, Standing Trunk Flexion Test, and shall have an average percentage degradation in distance of less than 25%.

5.4.1.2.14 LERL-4 ensembles shall be tested for gross body mobility as specified in Section 6.17, Upper Leg Flexion Test, and shall have an average percent degradation in range of motion of not less than 15%.

5.4.1.2.15 LERL-4 ensembles shall be tested for gross body mobility as specified in Section 6.18, Kneel and Rise Test, and the subject shall be able to rise from a kneeling position without assistance.

5.4.1.2.16 LERL-4 ensembles shall be tested for overall range of motion and functionality during a timed motion routine as specified in Section 6.20, Perimeter Scenario Test, and shall have an average percent degradation in time of less than 25%. Completion of all specified tasks is required. Ensembles shall not demonstrate any visible breach of integrity.

5.4.1.2.17 LERL-4 hand protection elements shall be tested for hand function as specified in Section 6.36, Glove Hand Function Test, and shall have an overall percentage degradation over bare-handed manipulation of less than 35%. Ensembles shall not demonstrate any visible breach of integrity.

5.4.1.2.18 LERL-4 hand protection elements shall be tested for fine dexterity (hand manipulation) as specified in Section 6.37, Fine Finger Dexterity Test, and shall have an average percentage degradation over bare-handed manipulation of less than 50%. Ensembles shall not demonstrate any visible breach of integrity.

5.4.1.2.19 LERL-4 garments with the associated respiratory protection shall be tested as specified in Section 6.43, Field of View Test, and shall obtain a VFS of 90 or greater.

5.4.1.3 LERL-4 ensembles shall be tested for liquid penetration resistance as specified in Section 6.41, Overall Liquid Integrity Test, and shall show no liquid penetration following a two-minute exposure.

5.4.1.4 LERL-4 ensembles shall be tested for audible signature as specified in Section 6.33, Audible Signature Test, and shall have an audible signature of 45 dBA or less.

5.4.2 **Garment Requirements for LERL-4 Ensemble Models**

5.4.2.1 LERL-4 garment materials and seams shall be tested for permeation resistance as specified in Section 6.22, Chemical Permeation Resistance Test, and shall meet the following performance criteria:[A]

- For permeation testing of HD, the cumulative permeation in one hour shall not exceed 4.0 $\mu g/cm^2$ for each specimen tested.

- For permeation testing of GD, the cumulative permeation in one hour shall not exceed 1.25 $\mu g/cm^2$ for each specimen tested.

- For permeation testing of liquid and gaseous TICs, the cumulative permeation in one hour shall not exceed 6.0 $\mu g/cm^2$ for each specimen tested for the chemicals listed in Sections 6.22.3.3 and 6.22.3.4.

5.4.2.2 LERL-4 garment materials and seams shall be tested for resistance to liquid or bloodborne pathogens as specified in Section 6.24, Viral Penetration Resistance Test, and shall allow no penetration of the Phi-X174 bacteriophage for one hour.[A]

5.4.2.3 LERL-4 garment material composites and seams shall be tested for resistance to liquid penetration under pressure as specified in Section 6.25, Expulsion Test, and shall allow no penetration for one hour using MeS.

5.4.2.4 LERL-4 garment material composites and seams shall be tested for resistance to liquid penetration when driven by rain as specified in Section 6.26, Rain Cabinet Test, and shall allow no penetration for one hour using TEP simulant.

5.4.2.5 LERL-4 woven garment materials shall be tested for tearing strength as specified in Section 6.27, Tearing Strength Test, and shall have a tear strength of not less than 30 N (7 lbf). [E]

5.4.2.6 LERL-4 garment materials shall be tested for cold weather performance as specified in Section 6.28, Cold Temperature Performance Test, and shall demonstrate no visible damage. [E]

5.4.2.7 LERL-4 nonwoven garment materials shall be tested for bursting strength as specified in Section 6.29, Burst Strength Test, and shall have a bursting strength of not less than 210 N (47 lbf). [A, E]

5.4.2.8 LERL-4 garment seams/closures shall be tested for seam strength as specified in Section 6.30, Seam/Closure Breaking Strength Test, and shall have a breaking strength of not less than 350 N (79 lbf). [A]

5.4.2.9 LERL-4 garment materials shall be tested for cut resistance as specified in Section 6.31, Cut Resistance Test, and shall have a cut resistance blade travel of not less than 25 mm (1 in) with a weight of 200 grams (7 oz). [A, E]

5.4.2.10 LERL-4 garment materials shall be tested for puncture resistance as specified in Section 6.32, Puncture Resistance Test, and shall have a puncture resistance of not less than 10 N (2 lbf). [E]

5.4.2.11 LERL-4 garment composites shall be tested for total heat loss as specified in Section 6.34, Total Heat Loss Test, and shall have a total heat loss equal to or greater than 450 W/m^2. [A]

5.4.2.12 LERL-4 garment composites shall be tested for flammability as specified in Section 6.5, Flame Impingement Test, and shall demonstrate no afterflame, no melt and no drip after the initial three-second exposure.

5.4.2.13 LERL-4 garment outer materials shall be tested for color/visibility in accordance with Section 6.44 and shall have a Y brightness value less than 25 and an L* value less than 55.

5.4.3 **Hand Protection Element Requirements for LERL-4 Ensemble Models**

5.4.3.1 Hand protection element types (gloves and glove liners) may be tested individually or in combination in order to meet the performance requirements outlined in this section.

- Where the hand protection element is composed of a single type of hand protection element, that element type shall meet all requirements of this section.

- Where the hand protection element is composed of multiple types of hand protection elements:
  o The outermost element type shall meet the requirements for cut resistance (Section 5.4.3.6), puncture resistance (Section 5.4.3.7), grip test (Section 5.4.3.99), flammability (Section 5.4.3.133) and color/visibility (Section 5.4.3.144).
  o The ensemble manufacturer shall indicate which of the element types is intended to meet the remaining requirements of this section.

5.4.3.2 LERL-4 hand protection element materials and seams shall be tested for permeation resistance as specified in Section 6.22, Chemical Permeation Resistance Test, and shall meet the following performance criteria:[A]

- For permeation testing of HD, the cumulative permeation in one hour shall not exceed 4.0 $\mu g/cm^2$ for each specimen tested.

- For permeation testing of GD, the cumulative permeation in one hour shall not exceed 1.25 $\mu g/cm^2$ for each specimen tested.

- For permeation testing of liquid and gaseous TICs, the cumulative permeation in one hour shall not exceed 6.0 $\mu g/cm^2$ for each specimen tested for the chemicals listed in Sections 6.22.3.3 and 6.22.3.4.

5.4.3.3 LERL-4 hand protection element materials and seams shall be tested for resistance to liquid or bloodborne pathogens as specified in Section 6.24, Viral Penetration Resistance Test, and shall allow no penetration of the Phi-X174 bacteriophage for one hour.[A]

5.4.3.4 LERL-4 hand protection element material composites and seams shall be tested for resistance to liquid penetration under pressure as specified in Section 6.25, Expulsion Test, and shall allow no penetration for one hour using MeS.

5.4.3.5 LERL-4 hand protection element material composites and seams shall be tested for resistance to liquid penetration when driven by rain as specified in Section 6.26, Rain Cabinet Test, and shall allow no penetration for one hour using TEP simulant.

5.4.3.6 LERL-4 hand protection element materials shall be tested for cut resistance as specified in Section 6.31, Cut Resistance Test, and shall have a cut resistance blade travel of not less than 25 mm (1 in) with a weight of 200 grams (7 oz).[A]

5.4.3.7 LERL-4 hand protection element materials shall be tested for puncture resistance as specified in Section 6.32, Puncture Resistance Test, and shall have a puncture resistance of not less than 15 N (4 lbf).[A]

5.4.3.8 LERL-4 hand protection element materials shall be tested for cold weather performance as specified in Section 6.28, Cold Temperature Performance Test, and shall demonstrate no visible damage.

5.4.3.9 LERL-4 hand protection elements shall be tested for grip as specified in Section 6.38, Grip Test, and shall have a weight-pulling capacity not less than 95% of the bare-hand control values.

5.4.3.10 LERL-4 hand protection element seams shall be tested for seam strength as specified in Section 6.30, Seam/Closure Breaking Strength Test, and shall have a breaking strength of not less than 350 N (79 lbf). [A]

5.4.3.11 LERL-4 nonwoven hand protection element materials shall be tested for bursting strength as specified in Section 6.29, Burst Strength Test, and shall have a bursting strength of not less than 210 N (47 lbf). [A]

5.4.3.12 LERL-4 woven hand protection element materials shall be tested for tearing strength as specified in Section 6.27, Tearing Strength Test, and shall have a tear strength of not less than 30 N (7 lbf).

5.4.3.13 LERL-4 hand protection element composites shall be tested for flammability as specified in Section 6.5, Flame Impingement Test, and shall demonstrate no afterflame, no melt and no drip after the initial three-second exposure.

5.4.3.14 LERL-4 hand protection element outer materials shall be tested for color/visibility in accordance with Section 6.44, Color/Visibility Test Method, and shall have a Y brightness value less than 25 and an L* value less than 55.

5.4.4 Foot Protection Element Requirements for LERL-4 Ensemble Models

5.4.4.1 Foot protection element types (footwear, footwear liners and footwear covers) may be tested individually or in combination in order to meet the performance requirements outlined in this section.

- Where the foot protection element is composed of a single type of foot protection element, that element type shall meet all requirements of this section.

- Where the foot protection element is composed of multiple types of foot protection elements:
    - The outermost element type shall meet the requirements for cut resistance (Section 5.4.4.6), puncture resistance (Section 5.4.4.7), abrasion resistance (Section 5.4.4.8), slip resistance (Section 5.4.4.9) and flammability (Section 5.4.4.10).
    - The ensemble manufacturer shall indicate which of the element types is intended to meet the remaining requirements of this section.

5.4.4.2 The appropriate LERL-4 foot protection element materials and seams shall be tested for permeation resistance as specified in Section 6.22, Chemical Permeation Resistance Test, and shall meet the following performance criteria: [A]

- For permeation testing of HD, the cumulative permeation in one hour shall not exceed 4.0 $\mu g/cm^2$ for each specimen tested.

- For permeation testing of GD, the cumulative permeation in one hour shall not exceed 1.25 $\mu g/cm^2$ for each specimen tested.

- For permeation testing of liquid and gaseous TICs, the cumulative permeation in one hour shall not exceed 6.0 $\mu g/cm^2$ for each specimen tested for the chemicals listed in Sections 6.22.3.3 and 6.22.3.4.

5.4.4.3   The appropriate LERL-4 foot protection element materials and seams shall be tested for resistance to liquid or bloodborne pathogens as specified in Section 6.24, Viral Penetration Resistance Test, and shall allow no penetration of the Phi-X174 bacteriophage for one hour.[A]

5.4.4.4   The appropriate LERL-4 foot protection element materials and seams shall be tested for resistance to liquid penetration under pressure as specified in Section 6.25, Expulsion Test, and shall allow no penetration for one hour using MeS.

5.4.4.5   The appropriate LERL-4 foot protection element materials and seams shall be tested for resistance to liquid penetration when driven by rain as specified in Section 6.26, Rain Cabinet Test, and shall allow no penetration for one hour using TEP simulant.

5.4.4.6   The appropriate LERL-4 foot protection element materials shall be tested for cut resistance as specified in Section 6.31, Cut Resistance Test, and shall have a cut resistance blade travel of not less than 25 mm (1 in) with a weight of 200 grams (7 oz).[A]

5.4.4.7   The appropriate LERL-4 foot protection element materials shall be tested for puncture resistance as specified in Section 6.32, Puncture Resistance Test, and shall have a puncture resistance of not less than 36 N (8 lbf).[A]

5.4.4.8   The appropriate LERL-4 foot protection element soles and heels shall be tested for abrasion resistance as specified in Section 6.39, Abrasion Resistance Test, and have an abrasion resistance rating of not less than 65.[A]

5.4.4.9   The appropriate LERL-4 foot protection element soles and heels shall be tested for slip resistance as specified in Section 6.42, Slip Resistance Test, and shall have a static coefficient of 0.75 or greater.[A]

5.4.4.10   The appropriate LERL-4 foot protection element materials shall be tested for flammability as specified in Section 6.5, Flame Impingement Test, and shall demonstrate no afterflame, no melt and no drip after the initial three-second exposure.

5.4.4.11   The appropriate LERL-4 foot protection element outer materials shall be tested for color/visibility in accordance with Section 6.44 and shall have a Y brightness value less than 25 and an L* value less than 55.

6. TEST METHODS

6.1 General

6.1.1 Performance requirement pass/fail criteria shall be as stated in Chapter 5, Performance Requirements.

6.1.2 Many conditioning procedures and test methods within this chapter reference other standards and test methods, such as those from the military, ASTM or NFPA.

6.1.2.1 Where a conditioning procedure or test method in this chapter references another document, the version referenced in Chapter 2 of this standard shall be used.

6.1.2.2 When the number of specimens is not specified within a test method of this standard, refer to the test method in the referenced document.

6.1.3 Unless the performance requirement is specifically stated as an average result, failure of any individual specimen result to meet the performance requirement shall constitute failing performance.

6.1.4 In this chapter, the term "ensemble" shall be understood to mean "CBRN protective ensemble."

6.1.5 Unless the context unmistakably indicates otherwise, the duration specified in this chapter for any procedure (e.g., "500 hours") shall be understood to run consecutively (e.g., "500 consecutive hours").

6.1.6 Unless the context unmistakably indicates otherwise, an indication that an action is to "follow" something else or otherwise is to occur after something else, should be understood to mean that the subsequent action should occur immediately after the preceding event.

6.1.7 Unless the test specifically states that facsimile samples may or must be used, facsimile samples shall not be used.

6.1.8 All samples and facsimile samples for testing shall be provided by the ensemble manufacturer.

6.1.9 For all tests requiring a test subject to use an SCBA, the ensemble manufacturer shall specify the size of the cylinder to be used.

6.1.10 For all tests requiring a test subject to perform tasks, a warm-up period is required immediately prior to the first test. Warm-up activities will consist of marching in place for one minute, 15 deep-knee bends, swinging the arms (forward and backward) for 30 seconds in each direction and 30 jumping jacks followed by a 10-minute rest period.

6.1.11 The size and weight of the test subject(s) for each test requiring a test subject shall be recorded.

6.2 Sample Conditioning Procedures

6.2.1 Room Temperature Conditioning

6.2.1.1 Samples shall be conditioned at a temperature of 21°C ± 3°C (70°F ± 5°F) and 65% ± 5% relative humidity (RH) in accordance with ASTM Standard D1776 for at least 24 hours. Specimens shall be tested within five minutes following removal from conditioning.[A]

6.2.2 Ensemble Conditioning

6.2.2.1 The ensemble conditioning protocol consists of the following sequence:

a) Hot diurnal environmental conditioning (see Section 6.2.3), followed by

b) Cold constant environmental conditioning (see Section 6.2.4), followed by

c) Humidity environmental conditioning (see Section 6.2.5), followed by

d) Vibration conditioning (see Section 6.2.6), followed by

e) Room temperature conditioning (see Section 6.2.1).

6.2.2.2 The entire ensemble, with the exception of the respiratory protection, shall undergo the protocol in the order stated in Section 6.2.2.1.

6.2.2.3 Each sample for conditioning shall be in new, unused condition and shall be in the packaging supplied by the ensemble manufacturer for normal field storage.

6.2.3 Hot Diurnal Environmental Conditioning

6.2.3.1 Hot diurnal environmental conditioning shall be performed in accordance with MIL-STD-810F, Method 501.4, Table 501.4-II, Hot Induced Conditions, with the following modifications[6]:

(1) Conditions shall be diurnal cycle, 35°C to 71°C (95°F to 160°F).

(2) Conditioning duration shall be 504 hours (three weeks).

6.2.4 Cold Constant Environmental Conditioning

6.2.4.1 Cold constant environmental conditioning shall be performed in accordance with MIL-STD-810F, Method 502.4 Low Temperature, with the following modifications:[7]

(1) Conditions shall be basic cold (C1), –32°C (–26°F) constant.

---

[6] *Statement of Standard for CBRN Full Facepiece Air Purifying Respirators (APR).* 2003. Washington, DC: NIOSH.

[7] *Statement of Standard for CBRN Full Facepiece Air Purifying Respirators (APR).* 2003. Washington, DC: NIOSH.

(2) Conditioning duration shall be 72 hours (three days).

6.2.5 Humidity Environmental Conditioning

6.2.5.1 Humidity environmental conditioning shall be performed in accordance with MIL-STD-810E, Method 507.3, Table 507.3-II, Hot Induced Conditions, with the following modifications.

(1) Conditions shall be natural cycle, cycle 1, diurnal cycle, 31°C (88°F), 88% RH to 41°C (105°F), 59% RH.

(2) Conditioning duration shall be 120 hours (five days).

6.2.6 Vibration Conditioning

6.2.6.1 Vibration conditioning shall be performed in accordance with MIL-STD-810F, Method 514.5, Vibration with modifications specified below.[8]

(1) Conditions shall be as indicated in MIL-STD-810F, Figure 514.5C-1, *U.S. highway truck vibration exposure.*

(2) Conditioning duration shall be 12 hours per axis for three axes with a total duration of 36 hours (equivalent to 12,000 miles).

6.2.7 Swatch Conditioning Protocol

6.2.7.1 The swatch conditioning protocol consists of the following sequence:

a) Hot diurnal environmental conditioning (see Section 6.2.3), followed by

b) Cold constant environmental conditioning (see Section 6.2.4), followed by

c) Humidity environmental conditioning (Section 6.2.5), followed by

d) Vibration conditioning (Section 6.2.6).

6.3 Sample Preparation

6.3.1 Application

6.3.1.1 This procedure shall apply as specified in Section 6.22, Chemical Permeation Resistance Test; Section 6.23, LERL-1 Toxic Industrial Chemical Permeation Resistance Test; Section 6.24, Viral Penetration Resistance Test; Section 6.25, Expulsion Test; and Section 6.26, Rain Cabinet Test.

6.3.1.2 Specific requirements for preparation of garment material samples shall be as described in Section 6.3.2.

---

[8] *Statement of Standard for CBRN Full Facepiece Air Purifying Respirators (APR).* 2003. Washington, DC: NIOSH.

6.3.1.3 Specific requirements for preparation of hand protection element material samples shall be as described in Section 6.3.3.

6.3.1.4 Specific requirements for preparation of foot protection upper material samples shall be as described in Section 6.3.4.

6.3.1.5 Specific requirements for preparation of foot protection element sole material samples shall be as described in Section 6.3.5.

6.3.1.6 Specific requirements for preparation of seam material samples shall be as described in Section 6.3.6.

6.3.2 **Garment Material Sample Preparation**

6.3.2.1 Samples for conditioning shall be taken from garment elements and shall be 200 mm x 280 mm (8 in x 11 in).

6.3.2.2 Samples shall be conditioned in accordance with the swatch conditioning protocol, Section 6.2.7.

6.3.2.3 Samples shall then be subjected to flexural fatigue in accordance with ASTM Standard F392 with the following modifications:

(1) In lieu of flexing conditions A, B, C, D or E, samples shall have a flex period of 200 cycles at 45 cycles per minute. A cycle shall be full flex and twisting action.

(2) Anisotropic materials shall be flexed in both machine and transverse directions.

(3) All layers of composites shall be present and intact during flex conditioning.

6.3.2.4 Following flexing, samples shall be abraded in accordance with ASTM Standard D4157, under the following conditions and with the following modifications:

(1) A 2.3 kg (5 lb) tension weight shall be used.

(2) A 1.6 kg (3.5 lb) head weight shall be used.

(3) Silicon carbide, ultrafine, 600 grit sandpaper shall be used as the abradant.

(4) The sample shall be abraded for 20 continuous cycles.

(5) The composite, with all layers present and intact, shall be subjected to this abrasion conditioning.

6.3.2.5 Following flexing and abrading, a specimen shall be taken from the center of each sample for testing, and the specimen shall be as shown in Figure 2.[A] Specimens shall be treated prior to testing as follows:

(1) Each specimen shall be treated with Break-Free® CLP® gun lubricant and synthetic sweat as specified in TOP 8-2-501, Appendix D.

(2) The gun lubricant shall be applied to the normal outer surface of the specimen (as worn).

(3) The synthetic sweat shall be applied to the normal inner surface of the specimen (as worn).

Figure 2. Specimen Dimensions

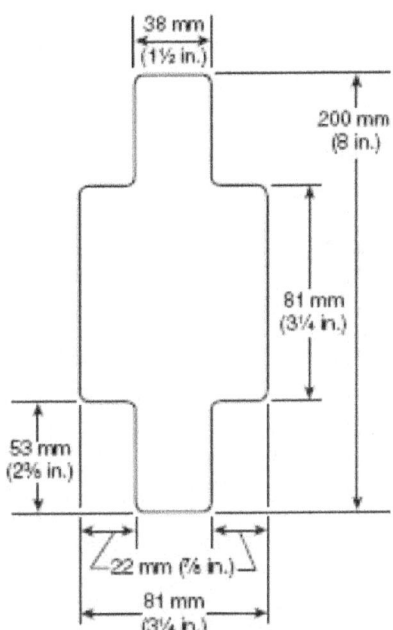

6.3.2.6   The specimens shall then be subjected to the appropriate test.

6.3.3   **Hand Protection Element Material Sample Preparation**

6.3.3.1   Samples for conditioning shall be whole hand protection elements. Facsimile samples shall not be used.

6.3.3.2   Samples shall be conditioned in accordance with the ensemble conditioning protocol, Section 6.2.1.1.

6.3.3.3   Sample hand protection elements shall be conditioned by having a test subject don the hand protection elements and perform the Fine Finger Dexterity Test steps of Section 6.37.4.2 twice.

6.3.3.4   All layers of composites shall be present and intact during dexterity conditioning.

6.3.3.5   Following dexterity conditioning, one specimen shall be taken from the center of each sample for testing. Specimens shall be treated prior to testing as follows:

(1) Each specimen shall be treated with Break-Free® CLP® gun lubricant and synthetic sweat as specified in TOP 8-2-501, Appendix D.

(2) The gun lubricant shall be applied to the normal outer surface of the specimen (as worn).

(3) The synthetic sweat shall be applied to the normal inner surface of the specimen (as worn).

6.3.3.6 The specimens shall then be subjected to the appropriate test.

6.3.4 Foot Protection Element Upper Material Sample Preparation

6.3.4.1 Where the foot protection element incorporates an element type constructed of garment material, garment material sample preparation as specified in Section 6.3.2 may be substituted for this sample preparation.

6.3.4.2 Samples for conditioning shall be complete foot protection elements. Facsimile samples shall not be used.

6.3.4.3 Samples shall be conditioned in accordance with the ensemble conditioning protocol, Section 6.2.1.1.

6.3.4.4 Sample foot protection elements shall be subjected to 20,000 flexes in accordance with FIA 1209, Whole Shoe Flex[9]. Water shall not be used in the flex procedure.

6.3.4.5 Following flexing, samples shall be taken in areas from the foot protection upper where the greatest flexing occurred and shall be abraded in accordance with ASTM Standard D4157 under the following conditions and with the following modifications:

(1) A 2.3 kg (5 lb) tension weight shall be used.

(2) A 1.6 kg (3.5 lb) head weight shall be used.

(3) Silicon carbide, ultrafine, 600 grit sandpaper shall be used as the abradant.

(4) The sample shall be abraded for 20 continuous cycles.

(5) The composite, with all layers present and intact, shall be subjected to this abrasion conditioning.

6.3.4.6 Following flexing and abrading, a specimen shall be taken from the center of each sample for testing, and specimens shall be as shown in Figure 2. Specimens shall be treated prior to testing as follows:

(1) Each specimen shall be treated with Break-Free® CLP® gun lubricant and synthetic sweat as specified in TOP 8-2-501, Appendix D.

(2) The gun lubricant shall be applied to the normal outer surface of the specimen (as worn).

---

[9] Referenced from NFPA 1999, *Standard on Protective Clothing for Emergency Medical Operations.* 2003.

(3) The synthetic sweat shall be applied to the normal inner surface of the specimen (as worn).

6.3.4.7 The specimens shall then be subjected to the appropriate test.

6.3.5 **Foot Protection Element Sole Material Sample Preparation**

6.3.5.1 Where the foot protection element incorporates an element type constructed of garment material, garment material sample preparation as specified in Section 6.3.2 may be substituted for this sample preparation.

6.3.5.2 Samples for conditioning shall be sole material samples or facsimile samples at least 81 mm x 200 mm (3.25 in x 8 in).

6.3.5.3 Samples shall be conditioned in accordance with the swatch conditioning protocol, Section 6.2.7.

6.3.5.4 Where the sole composition is a thermoplastic material, samples shall be from the actual sole of the foot protection element or shall be compression-molded facsimile samples with a consistent thickness from the thermoplastic compound used to manufacture the foot protection element sole.

6.3.5.5 Where the sole composition is vulcanized rubber, samples shall be compression-molded facsimile samples with a consistent thickness from the nonvulcanized compound used to manufacture the foot protection sole.

6.3.5.6 Where the sole composition is a thermoset material, samples shall be compression-molded facsimile samples with a consistent thickness from the thermoset material used to manufacture the foot protection sole.

6.3.5.7 Facsimile sole samples shall be of a maximum thickness representative of the thinnest portion of the sole, exclusive of hardware, midsoles or inner soles.

6.3.5.8 Samples shall be abraded in accordance with ASTM Standard D4157 under the following conditions and with the following modifications:

(1) A 2.3 kg (5 lb) tension weight shall be used.

(2) A 1.6 kg (3.5 lb) head weight shall be used.

(3) Silicon carbide, ultrafine, 600 grit sandpaper shall be used as the abradant.

(4) The sample shall be abraded for 20 continuous cycles.

(5) The composite, with all layers present and intact, shall be subjected to this abrasion conditioning.

6.3.5.9 Following abrading, one specimen shall be taken from the center of each sample for testing, and the specimen shall be as shown in Figure 2. Specimens shall be treated prior to testing as follows:

(1) Each specimen shall be treated with Break-Free® CLP® gun lubricant and synthetic sweat as specified in TOP 8-2-501, Appendix D.

(2) The gun lubricant shall be applied to the normal outer surface of the specimen (as worn).

(3) The synthetic sweat shall be applied to the normal inner surface of the specimen.

6.3.5.10   The specimens shall then be subjected to the appropriate test.

6.3.6   **Seam Sample Preparation**

6.3.6.1   Garment element, hand protection element, foot protection element, garment-to-element or garment-to-visor seam samples, including facsimile samples, may be used.

6.3.6.1.1   If seam samples are used, the samples shall be taken from each different type of seam found in the ensemble.

6.3.6.1.2   If facsimile samples are used, the facsimile samples shall represent each different type of seam found in the ensemble.

6.3.6.1.3   Hand protection element seam samples shall be taken from the gauntlet (i.e., wrist/arm portion) of the hand protection element when an external seam is used in the construction of the hand protection element.

6.3.6.2   Samples for conditioning shall be 600 mm (23.5 in) lengths of facsimile samples.

6.3.6.3   Samples shall be conditioned in accordance with the swatch conditioning protocol, Section 6.2.7.

6.3.6.4   Specimens shall be taken from seam samples that have a minimum of 75 mm (3 in) of material on each side of the seam center.

6.3.6.5   Specimens shall be cut such that the exact seam center divides the specimen in half. Specimens shall be treated as follows:

(1) Each specimen shall be treated with Break-Free® CLP® gun lubricant and synthetic sweat as specified in TOP 8-2-501, Appendix D.

(2) The gun lubricant shall be applied to the normal outer surface of the specimen (as worn).

(3) The synthetic sweat shall be applied to the normal inner surface of the specimen (as worn).

6.3.6.6   The specimens shall then be subjected to the appropriate test.

6.4   **Man-In-Simulant Test (MIST)**

6.4.1   ASTM Standard F2588 shall be applied with the following modifications:

(1) Samples will consist of the complete ensemble, including respiratory protection.

(2) The samples shall consist of four ensembles, consisting of two different sizes for men and two different sizes for women, for each model of respiratory protection with which the ensemble model is to be tested for compliance.

(3) Samples shall be conditioned in accordance with the ensemble conditioning protocol (see Section 6.2.1.1) prior to testing.

(4) The Rest 1 portion of ASTM Standard F2588, Section 12.3.5.9, shall be replaced with lying prone on the floor, facing the wind and simulating weapon sighting and firing sequence for one minute.

6.4.2   Specimens shall be the conditioned samples.

6.5   **Flame Impingement**

6.5.1   ASTM Standard F1358 shall be applied with the following modifications:

(1) Samples shall be conditioned in accordance with the room temperature conditioning protocol (see Section 6.2.1) prior to testing.

(2) Only the three-second exposure time shall be used for testing.

(3) The flame shall be applied to the side of the specimen corresponding to the exterior surface of the ensemble element.

6.6   **Donning and Doffing Test[F, 10]**

6.6.1   **Application**

6.6.1.1 This test method shall apply to all ensembles, regardless of LERL.

6.6.2   **Samples**

6.6.2.1 Four complete ensembles are required as samples, consisting of two different sizes for men and two different sizes for women, for each model of respiratory protection with which the ensemble model is to be tested for compliance. Samples shall be provided to fit, or to be adjustable to fit, the test subjects in accordance with the ensemble manufacturer's sizing provisions specific to each ensemble.

6.6.2.2 Samples shall consist of ensembles including the garments, hand protection elements, foot protection elements and the respiratory protection specified by the ensemble manufacturer.

---

[10] All subsections of 6.6 are derived from *Proposed Specifications for a Performance Standard for Chemical and Biological Protective Clothing and Equipment for Law Enforcement Operations* (see Table 5, Letter F of this document.)

6.6.2.3 Samples shall be conditioned in accordance with the ensemble conditioning protocol (see Section 6.2.1.1) prior to testing.

6.6.3 Procedure

6.6.3.1 Test subjects shall be clothed initially in long pants, tee shirt, socks and tactical boots.

6.6.3.2 Subjects shall review the donning, doffing and adjustment procedures provided by the ensemble manufacturer and by the respiratory protection manufacturer prior to the start of the test.

6.6.3.2.1 Nontest samples may be examined prior to the actual test. Practice cycles may be performed on nontest samples to familiarize the subject with donning, doffing and adjustment procedures.

6.6.3.3 The donning test shall begin with the subject sitting in an armless chair with the packaged ensemble in front.

6.6.3.4 At a cue from the test administrator, the subject shall rise from the chair and begin donning the ensemble in accordance with the ensemble manufacturer's instructions. Timing shall start at the cue from the administrator.

6.6.3.5 The subject shall don the ensemble unassisted. The chair shall be permitted to be used during the process.

6.6.3.6 At the completion of donning, the subject shall cue the test administrator.

6.6.3.7 Timing shall cease at the cue from the subject. The administrator shall note the donning time.

6.6.3.8 A visual fit and closure inspection by trained personnel shall be performed.[11]

6.6.3.9 The doffing test shall begin with the subject wearing the properly donned ensemble and sitting in the armless chair.

6.6.3.10 At a cue from the test administrator, the subject shall rise from the chair and begin doffing the ensemble in accordance with the ensemble manufacturer's instructions. Timing shall commence at the cue from the administrator.

6.6.3.11 The subject shall doff the ensemble unassisted. The chair may be used during the process.

6.6.3.12 At the completion of doffing, the subject shall cue the test administrator. Doffing is completed when the test subject is seated wearing long pants, tee shirt, socks and tactical boots.

---

[11] The gross body mobility tests (see Section 6.7) may be performed between the donning and doffing tests.

6.6.3.13 Timing shall cease at the cue from the subject. The administrator shall note the doffing time.

6.6.3.14 The administrator shall inspect the ensemble and note any deficiencies in the doffing of the ensemble.

6.6.4 Report

6.6.4.1 The donning and doffing times for each specimen shall be recorded and reported.

6.6.4.2 The average donning and doffing times for all specimens shall be recorded and reported.

6.6.4.3 Any visible breach of integrity shall be reported.

6.6.5 Interpretation

6.6.5.1 Any visible breach of integrity shall constitute failing results.

6.7 Gross Body Mobility Tests [F,12,13]

6.7.1 Individual Tests

The gross body mobility tests consist of the following:

- Forward walking test (see Section 6.8).

- Backward walking test (see Section 6.9).

- Side step walking test (see Section 6.10).

- Upper arm abduction test (see Section 6.11).

- Upper arm forward extension test (see Section 6.12).

- Upper arm backward extension test (see Section 6.13).

- Upper leg forward extension test (see Section 6.14).

- Upper leg backward extension test (see Section 6.15).

- Standing trunk flexion test (see Section 6.16).

- Upper leg flexion test (see Section 6.17).

- Kneel and rise test (see Section 6.18).

---

[12] All subsections of 6.7 and the test methods referred to therein are derived from *Proposed Specifications for a Performance Standard for Chemical and Biological Protective Clothing and Equipment for Law Enforcement Operations* (see Table 5, Letter F of this document.)

[13] The gross body mobility tests may be performed between the donning and doffing tests.

6.7.2   **General Procedure**

6.7.2.1   The test subject shall be clothed initially in long pants, tee shirt, socks and tactical boots.

6.7.2.2   The subject shall don the ensemble per the ensemble manufacturer's instructions and shall perform each individual test procedure listed in Section 6.7.1 three consecutive times with the result of each test being an average of the three trials.

6.7.2.3   The test subject shall stand erect during each test.

6.7.2.4   For each gross body mobility test requiring a test subject to perform repetitive motion with a limb, the same limb shall be used for each repetition.

6.7.2.5   Following the completion of all test procedures listed in Section 6.7.1, the subject shall doff the ensemble.

6.7.2.6   Measurements or observations shall be recorded for each trial of each mobility test as specified. Linear measurements shall be recorded to the nearest centimeter. Angular measurements shall be recorded to the nearest degree.

6.7.2.7   Any visible breach of integrity of the ensemble shall be reported and shall constitute failing results.

6.7.3   **Application**

6.7.3.1   Gross body mobility tests shall apply to all ensembles, regardless of law enforcement response level.

6.7.4   **Samples**

6.7.4.1   Four complete ensembles, consisting of two different sizes for men and two different sizes for women, are required as samples for testing. Samples shall be provided to fit, or to be adjustable to fit, the test subjects in accordance with the ensemble manufacturer's sizing provisions specific to each ensemble.

6.7.4.2   Samples shall consist of ensembles including the garments, hand protection elements, foot protection elements and the respiratory protection specified by the ensemble manufacturer.

6.7.4.3   Samples shall be conditioned in accordance with the ensemble conditioning protocol (see Section 6.2.1.1) prior to testing.

6.7.4.4   The specimens shall be tested with each model of respiratory protection specified by the ensemble manufacturer.

6.7.5   Calculation

6.7.5.1   The percent degradation as applicable for each gross body mobility test shall be calculated using Equation 1:

Equation 1. Percent Degradation

$$X = \frac{D1 - D2}{D1} \times 1 0$$

Where:
X = Percent degradation of joint movement, or distance covered.
$D1$ = Measured joint angular rotation (degrees) or distance (cm) wearing loose-fitting clothing.
$D2$ = Measured joint angular rotation (degrees) or distance (cm) wearing the ensemble.

6.8   Forward Walking Test[F]

6.8.1   Procedure

6.8.1.1   The subject shall take five steps forward, each as far forward as possible, bringing the feet together after each step. The subject shall lead each step with alternating feet.

6.8.2   Measurement

6.8.2.1   The distance traveled shall be measured and recorded from the heel of the foot when starting to the toe of the foot taking the fifth step.

6.9   Backward Walking Test[F]

6.9.1   Procedure

6.9.1.1   The subject shall take five steps backward, each as far backward as possible, bringing the feet together after each step. The subject shall lead each step with alternating feet.

6.9.2   Measurement

6.9.2.1   The distance traveled shall be measured and recorded from the toe of the foot when starting to the heel of the foot taking the fifth step.

6.10   Side Step Walking Test[F]

6.10.1   Procedure

6.10.1.1   The subject shall take five steps sideways in the left direction, each as far as possible, bringing the feet together after each step.

6.10.2   **Measurement**

6.10.2.1   The distance from the right side of the right foot when starting to the left side of the left foot after finishing the fifth step shall be measured and recorded.

6.11   **Upper Arm Abduction Test**[F]

6.11.1   **Procedure**

6.11.1.1   With arms at sides and palms facing the body, the subject shall raise the arms sideward and upward as far as possible. Elbows shall remain locked.

6.11.2   **Measurement**

6.11.2.1   The center of the goniometer shall be held even with the tested joint (the shoulder). The goniometer shall be held parallel to the axis of the bone being moved and perpendicular to the floor.

6.11.2.2   The maximum angular rotation of the joint shall be measured and recorded.

6.12   **Upper Arm Forward Extension Test**[F]

6.12.1   **Procedure**

6.12.1.1   With arms at sides and palms facing rear, the subject shall raise the arms forward and upward as far as possible. Elbows shall remain locked.

6.12.2   **Measurement**

6.12.2.1   The center of the goniometer shall be held even with the tested joint (the shoulder). The goniometer shall be held parallel to the axis of the bone being moved and perpendicular to the floor.

6.12.2.2   The maximum angular rotation of the joint shall be measured and recorded.

6.13   **Upper Arm Backward Extension Test**[F]

6.13.1   **Procedure**

6.13.1.1   With palms facing toward the rear, the subject shall raise the arm backward and upward as far as possible. Elbow shall remain locked.

6.13.1.2   The subject shall stand with chest against an external corner, door jamb or similar structure to prevent bending at the waist

6.13.2   **Measurement**

6.13.2.1   The center of the goniometer shall be held even with the tested joint (the shoulder). The goniometer shall be held parallel to the axis of the bone being moved and perpendicular to the floor.

6.13.2.2   The maximum angular rotation of the joint shall be measured and recorded.

6.14   **Upper Leg Forward Extension Test[F]**

6.14.1   **Procedure**

6.14.1.1   The subject shall raise a leg forward and upward as far as possible while keeping the knee locked.

6.14.1.2   The subject shall hold onto a support (such as the back of a chair) while performing this movement.

6.14.2   **Measurement**

6.14.2.1   The center of the goniometer shall be held even with the tested joint (the hip). The goniometer shall be held parallel to the axis of the bone being moved and perpendicular to the floor.

6.14.2.2   The maximum angular rotation of the joint shall be measured and recorded.

6.15   **Upper Leg Backward Extension Test[F]**

6.15.1   **Procedure**

6.15.1.1   The subject shall raise the leg backward and upward as far as possible. The knee shall remain locked.

6.15.1.2   The subject shall stand against a wall for support while performing this movement.

6.15.2   **Measurement**

6.15.2.1   The center of the goniometer shall be held even with the tested joint (the hip). The goniometer shall be held parallel to the axis of the bone being moved and perpendicular to the floor.

6.15.2.2   The maximum angular rotation of the joint shall be measured and recorded.

6.16   **Standing Trunk Flexion Test[F]**

6.16.1   **Procedure**

6.16.1.1   Beginning from an upright posture, the subject shall bend at the waist as far as possible without bending the knees while reaching the fingertips toward the floor.

6.16.2   Measurement

6.16.2.1   The distance from the tip of the middle finger to the floor shall be measured and recorded. The middle finger touching the floor shall be recorded as zero.

6.17   Upper Leg Flexion Test[F]

6.17.1   Procedure

6.17.1.1   The subject shall raise a leg as far upward (toward the chest) as possible, allowing the knee to bend freely.

6.17.1.2   The subject shall stand against a wall for support while performing this movement.

6.17.2   Measurement

6.17.2.1   The center of the goniometer shall be held even with the tested joint (the hip). The goniometer shall be held parallel to the axis of the bone being moved and perpendicular to the floor.

6.17.2.2   The maximum angular rotation of the joint shall be measured and recorded.

6.18   Kneel and Rise Test[F]

6.18.1   Procedure

6.18.1.1   Beginning from a standing position, the subject shall get down on both knees and stand up again.

6.18.1.2   A chair shall be provided for use as assistance if necessary.

6.18.1.3   The subject shall not be allowed to use hands to adjust the ensemble during kneeling.

6.18.2   Observation

The subject shall be observed for the ability to rise from a kneeling position without any assistance.

6.19   Tactical Scenario Test[F]

6.19.1   Application

6.19.1.1   This test shall apply to LERL-1, LERL-2 and LERL-3 ensembles.

6.19.2   Samples

6.19.2.1   Four complete ensembles are required as samples, consisting of two different sizes for men and two different sizes for women, for each model of respiratory protection with which the ensemble model is to be tested for compliance.

6.19.2.2 Samples shall be provided to fit, or to be adjustable to fit, the selected test subjects in accordance with the ensemble manufacturer's sizing provisions specific to each ensemble.

6.19.2.3 Samples shall be conditioned in accordance with the ensemble conditioning protocol (see Section 6.2.1.1) prior to testing.

6.19.3 Site Specifications

6.19.3.1 The tactical scenario test shall take place indoors under conditions within the following ranges: 20°C to 28°C (68°F to 82°F) and 30% to 70% RH. To mitigate potential heat stress, participants will be free to take rest breaks (timing shall not stop during any such breaks).

6.19.3.2 A staging area shall be available adjacent to the test area and shall be large enough to permit donning and doffing of the ensemble.

6.19.3.3 The test area shall consist of the following:

6.19.3.3.1 A staircase of at least 11 steps, leading down to a hallway and two rooms.

6.19.3.3.2 A straight run of at least 50 ft followed by a 4-ft scalable wall.

6.19.4 Required Props

6.19.4.1 The following equipment shall be provided:

- NIJ-compliant Level IV ballistic body armor[14] properly sized to each test subject.
- Tactical ballistic helmet (properly sized to each test subject).
- Shoulder weapon (Colt M4 Carbine) with an attached sling and an extra magazine on the vest.
- Side arm (Glock 17) on dropdown leg holster and magazine pouch on opposite legs, one magazine in weapon and two additional magazines in pouch.
- Flex cuffs.
- Portable radio (in pouch on vest).
- Mannequin: Simulaids Rescue Randy Model 1475 or equivalent (articulated, 6 ft, 1 in height, 165-lb weight).

---

[14] Ballistic body armor of a model found by NIJ to be compliant with the requirements of NIJ Standard-0101.06 for Level IV, or, if there is a revised or successor standard, with the requirements of such standard for such level or its equivalent.

6.19.5   Required Personnel

6.19.5.1 The following personnel shall be provided:

- Two male and two female test subjects.
    - For baseline time (Tb) determination: test subject wearing (inside to out) duty uniform, tactical vest with utility pouch and tactical helmet.
    - For time while wearing ensemble (Te) determination: test subject wearing duty uniform, ensemble with the ensemble manufacturer-specified respiratory protection, tactical vest with utility pouch and tactical helmet. For LERL-1 and LERL-2, the CBRN SCBA unit shall be worn over the tactical vest. For LERL-3, the PAPR unit shall be worn on the outside of the tactical vest.
- Individual for arrest scenario.
- Timekeeper.
- Data recorder/prompter.

6.19.6   Procedure

6.19.6.1 The following sequence is to be performed by each subject, first while wearing a duty uniform with required props to establish the baseline time and then while wearing the complete ensemble over the duty uniform.

6.19.6.1.1 Assemble at the staging area. The subject shall don the ensemble and required props and proceed to the top of the staircase.

6.19.6.1.2 The timekeeper shall give the "start" signal and begin timing.

6.19.6.1.3 With shoulder weapon presented at low ready, the subject shall descend the stairs.

6.19.6.1.4 The area beneath the stairs shall be open and unobstructed. At the bottom of the stairs, the subject shall visually clear the area adjacent to and beneath the stairs.

6.19.6.1.5 The subject shall open and pass through the door into the hallway. The subject shall visually clear the hallway and proceed to the door.

6.19.6.1.6 The subject shall open and pass through the door to the adjacent room. The room shall contain an individual standing 12 ft from the door.

6.19.6.1.7 The subject shall train the weapon on the individual until a sight picture (see 3.2.65) is obtained and verbally confirmed by the subject.

6.19.6.1.8 While keeping the weapon trained on the individual, the subject shall order the individual to kneel by stating:

"Place your hands on top of your head and drop down to your knees."

6.19.6.1.9 The subject shall drop the shoulder weapon (which will be caught by the sling) and draw and train the sidearm on the individual. The subject shall remove the magazine from the weapon, stow the magazine in the pouch, remove a new magazine from the pouch, insert the new magazine into the weapon and simulate chambering a round.

6.19.6.1.10 The subject shall approach and stand next to the individual and holster the weapon. The subject shall then use flex cuffs to restrain the individual's arms behind the back while giving appropriate commands as follows:

"Keep your left hand on your head."

6.19.6.1.11 The subject places a flex cuff on right wrist of the individual, secures it and moves the wrist to the small of the individual's back. Subject then grabs the individual's left hand and moves it to the small of the individual's back while stating:

"Bring your left hand down to your back."

6.19.6.1.12 The subject then secures the flex cuff around the left wrist.

6.19.6.1.13 The subject shall frisk the individual to ensure the individual is not armed and then shall assist the individual to a standing position.

6.19.6.1.14 The subject shall radio team members that one person is in custody and that the subject will be exiting the door with the restrained individual by stating:

"I have one in custody. I will be exiting the door with the prisoner."

6.19.6.1.15 The subject shall escort the individual through the door while grasping the individual by the arms or wrists.

6.19.6.1.16 The subject shall hand off the restrained individual to a team member outside and return to the room with the shoulder weapon presented at low ready. The subject shall then visually clear the area.

6.19.6.1.17 The subject shall re-enter the hallway, with the shoulder weapon drawn, and proceed to another door.

6.19.6.1.18 The subject shall enter the area through the door and visually clear the area. The area shall contain the rescue mannequin (downed officer).

6.19.6.1.19 The subject shall proceed toward the mannequin, drop the shoulder weapon (which will be caught by the sling) and extract the downed officer by lifting the mannequin under the arms and dragging it 10 ft.

6.19.6.1.20 The subject shall shoulder the weapon at low ready.

6.19.6.1.21 The subject shall shoulder the weapon in preparation to fire, obtain a sight picture and simulate firing two shots.

6.19.6.1.22 Simulating a malfunction, the subject shall clear the shoulder weapon by removing the magazine, inserting a second magazine and simulating chambering a round.

6.19.6.1.23 With the shoulder weapon at low ready, the subject shall proceed at a fast pace 50 ft to a 4-ft high wall. (A fast pace is considered to be a speed no faster than that at which the subject can accurately fire his weapon.)

6.19.6.1.24 The subject shall sling the shoulder weapon and scale the wall by climbing over it.

6.19.6.1.25 When both of the subject's feet are on the ground after scaling the wall, timing is complete and the timekeeper shall record the overall time.

6.19.6.1.26 The ensemble shall be examined for any visual breach of integrity prior to doffing.

6.19.6.1.27 The test subject shall doff the ensemble. Following doffing, the ensemble shall be examined for any visual breach of integrity.

6.19.7   Calculation

6.19.7.1   The percent degradation for the scenario test shall be calculated using Equation 2:

Equation 2. Percent Degradation for Tactical Scenario Test

$$X = \frac{Te - Tb}{Tb} \times 1\,0$$

Where:
X = Percent degradation for the entire scenario.
Tb = Baseline time (in seconds) for the entire scenario while wearing duty uniform.
Te = Time (in seconds) for the entire scenario while wearing ensemble.

6.19.7.2   Percent degradation shall be determined for each ensemble.

6.19.8   Report

6.19.8.1   The baseline time (Tb) shall be recorded and reported for each subject.

6.19.8.2   The ensemble time (Te) shall be recorded and reported for each subject wearing an ensemble.

6.19.8.3   The percent degradation (X) for each ensemble over the entire scenario shall be recorded and reported.

6.19.8.4   The average percent degradation (average of X) for all ensembles shall be recorded and reported.

6.19.8.5   Any visible breach of integrity of the ensemble prior to doffing shall be reported.

6.19.8.6   Any visible breach of integrity of the ensemble following doffing shall be reported.

6.19.8.7 Failure to complete any task shall be recorded and reported.

6.19.9 **Interpretation**

6.19.9.1 The average percent degradation (average of X) shall be used as the pass/fail criterion.

6.19.9.2 Any failure of the subject to complete a task due to ensemble restrictions shall constitute failing results.

6.19.9.3 Any visible breach of integrity of the ensemble prior to doffing shall constitute failing results.

6.19.9.4 Any visible breach of integrity of the ensemble following doffing shall constitute failing results.

6.20 **Perimeter Scenario Test[F]**

6.20.1 **Application**

6.20.1.1 This test shall apply to LERL-4 CBRN protective ensembles.

6.20.2 **Samples**

6.20.2.1 Four complete ensembles are required as samples, consisting of two different sizes for men and two different sizes for women, for each model of respiratory protection with which the ensemble model is to be tested for compliance.

6.20.2.2 Samples shall be provided to fit, or to be adjustable to fit, the test subjects in accordance with the ensemble manufacturer's sizing provisions specific to each ensemble.

6.20.2.3 Samples shall be conditioned in accordance with the ensemble conditioning protocol (see Section 6.2.1.1) prior to testing.

6.20.3 **Site Specifications**

6.20.3.1 The perimeter scenario test shall take place indoors under conditions within the following ranges: 20°C to 28°C (68°F to 82°F) and 30% to 70% RH. To mitigate potential heat stress, participants will be free to take rest breaks (timing shall not stop during any such breaks).

6.20.3.2 A staging area shall be available adjacent to the test area and shall be large enough to permit donning and doffing of the ensemble.

6.20.3.3 The test area shall consist of the following:

- Three posts at least 60 in high, separated by at least 20 ft, and of suitable diameter to allow for the attachment of barricade tape.

- One 27-in high guardrail or equivalent.
- Police barricade tape (two rolls, yellow, approximately 76 mm wide by 3 mm thick or similar, stored at staging area).

6.20.3.3.1 The basic setup of the test configuration is diagrammed in Figure 3.

Figure 3. Perimeter Scenario Test Configuration

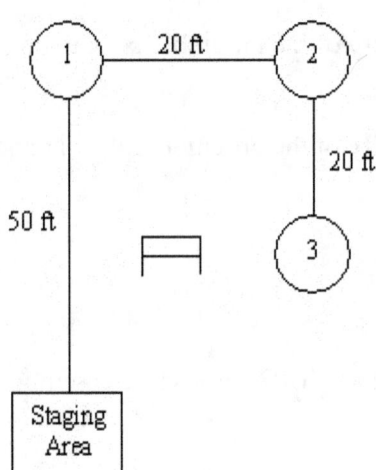

6.20.4 **Required Props**

6.20.4.1 The following equipment shall be provided:

- Sidearm (Glock 17) in dropdown leg holster and magazine pouch on opposite legs, one magazine in weapon and two additional magazines on duty belt.
- NIJ-compliant Level II ballistic body armor[15] properly sized to fit each test subject.
- Portable radio (in pouch on duty belt).
- Small notebook (on subject, if subject has pockets).
- Pen (on subject, if subject has pockets).
- First-aid kit containing elastic bandage (stored at staging area).
- Flashlight (on subject).
- Duty belt with handcuffs, two magazines, pepper spray, pouch and expandable baton.

---

[15] Ballistic body armor of a model found by NIJ to be compliant with the requirements of NIJ Standard-0101.06 for Level II, or, if there is a revised or successor standard, with the requirements of such standard for such level or its equivalent.

6.20.5   **Required Personnel**

6.20.5.1   The following personnel shall be provided:

- Two male and two female test subjects.
  - For baseline time (Tb) determination: test subject wearing (inside to out) personal body armor, duty uniform and duty belt.
  - For time while wearing ensemble (Te) determination: test subject wearing (inside to out) personal body armor, duty uniform, ensemble with ensemble manufacturer-specified respiratory protection and duty belt.

- Individual for victim scenario.

- Timekeeper.

- Data recorder/prompter.

- Individual to serve as a dispatcher.

6.20.6   **Procedure**

6.20.6.1   The following sequence is to be performed by each subject, first while wearing a duty uniform with the required props to establish the baseline time and then while wearing the complete ensemble over the duty uniform.

6.20.6.1.1 Assemble at the staging area. The subject shall don the ensemble and required props.

6.20.6.1.2 The timekeeper shall give the "start" signal and begin timing.

6.20.6.1.3 The subject shall retrieve the barricade tape and walk 50 ft from the staging area to Post 1.

6.20.6.1.4 The subject shall secure the barricade tape by tying it to Post 1 approximately 4 ft from the ground.

6.20.6.1.5 The subject shall walk to Post 2 while unrolling the barricade tape and then tie it to Post 2, thus setting up a secure area.

6.20.6.1.6 The subject shall return to the staging area, retrieve a second roll of barricade tape, return to Post 2 and secure barricade tape by tying it to Post 2.

6.20.6.1.7 The subject shall walk to Post 3 while unrolling the barricade tape and secure the barricade tape to Post 3 by tying it. Barricade tape should now be secured between Posts 1 and 2, and Posts 2 and 3.

6.20.6.1.8 The subject shall walk back to the staging area. On arrival, the subject shall use the radio and make a radio transmission. The subject shall manipulate the radio controls, provide a report of the scene, and deliver and receive commands as follows:

Subject: "Unit 1 to base."
Dispatcher: "Unit 1, proceed."

> Subject: "Unit 1, I have a suspected contaminated environment. I have one victim down. I will be checking further."
>
> Dispatcher: "Unit 1, okay."

6.20.6.1.9 The subject shall retrieve the notebook and pen. The subject shall write the alphabet and numerals 0-9. The notebook and pen shall then be stowed.

6.20.6.1.10 The subject shall walk to the barricade between Posts 2 and 3. Before reaching the barricade tape, the subject shall go over, under and then around the guardrail.

6.20.6.1.11 The subject shall proceed to the barricade, duck under the tape and walk 25 ft beyond the tape to the victim with an injured arm. The subject shall self-identify to the victim, ask the victim questions and receive the victim's reply as follows:

> Subject: "Are you injured?"
> Victim: "Yes, my upper arm is injured."
> Subject: "I am going to help you to the staging area."
> Victim: "Okay."

6.20.6.1.12 The subject shall escort the victim to the staging area.

6.20.6.1.13 At the staging area, the subject shall retrieve the first-aid kit and, using the elastic bandage, wrap the victim's upper arm.

6.20.6.1.14 The subject shall proceed to Post 2, draw the flashlight and weapon, power on the flashlight and pan the area beyond the barrier tape with both the weapon and the flashlight.

6.20.6.1.15 The subject shall stow the flashlight and weapon and proceed to Post 1.

6.20.6.1.16 The subject shall redraw the weapon, obtain a sight picture, speak the following command and simulate firing two shots:

"Police, do not move."

6.20.6.1.17 Simulating a malfunction, the subject shall remove the magazine from the weapon, stow the magazine, remove a new magazine from the duty belt, insert the new magazine into the weapon and simulate chambering a round. The subject shall then reholster the weapon.

6.20.6.1.18 The subject shall return to the staging area. On arrival, timing is complete.

6.20.6.1.19 The timekeeper shall record the time.

6.20.6.1.20 The ensemble shall be examined for any visual breach of integrity prior to doffing.

6.20.6.1.21 The test subject shall doff the ensemble. Following doffing, the ensemble shall be examined for any visual breach of integrity.

6.20.7   **Calculation**

6.20.7.1   The percent degradation of the ensemble shall be calculated using Equation 3:

Equation 3. Percent Degradation for Perimeter Scenario Test

$$X = \frac{Te - Tb}{Tb} \times 1'0$$

Where:
X = Percent degradation for the scenario.
Tb = Baseline time (seconds) while wearing duty uniform.
Te = Time (seconds) while wearing ensemble.

6.20.7.2   Percent degradation (X) shall be determined for the scenario.

6.20.8   **Report**

6.20.8.1   The baseline time (Tb) shall be recorded and reported for each subject.

6.20.8.2   The ensemble time (Te) shall be recorded and reported for each subject wearing an ensemble.

6.20.8.3   The percent degradation (X) for each ensemble over the entire scenario shall be calculated and reported.

6.20.8.4   The average percent degradation (average of X) for all ensembles shall be calculated and reported.

6.20.8.5   Any visible breach of integrity of the ensemble prior to doffing shall be reported.

6.20.8.6   Any visible breach of integrity of the ensemble following doffing shall be reported.

6.20.8.7   Failure to complete any individual task shall be reported.

6.20.9   **Interpretation**

6.20.9.1   The average percent degradation (average of X) of all ensembles tested shall be used as the pass/fail criterion.

6.20.9.2   Any failure of the subject to complete a task due to ensemble restrictions shall constitute failing results.

6.20.9.3   Any visible breach of integrity of the ensemble prior to doffing shall constitute failing results.

6.20.9.4   Any visible breach of integrity of the ensemble following doffing shall constitute failing results.

6.21   Flash Fire Test

6.21.1   Application

6.21.1.1   This method shall apply to LERL-1 ensembles.

6.21.1.2   Specimens shall be tested in accordance with ASTM Standard F1930 with the following modifications:

(1) Three complete ensembles are required as samples, with the exception that the respiratory protection is not required. Hand protection elements and foot protection elements shall be placed on the mannequin even though these areas of the mannequin are not instrumented.

(2) Samples shall be conditioned in accordance with the ensemble conditioning protocol in Section 6.2.1.1 of this standard prior to testing.

(3) A heat flux exposure of 84 kW/m^2 (2.02 cal/cm^2·sec) shall be used with an exposure time of three seconds.

(4) The mannequin shall be dressed in 150 g/m^2 ± 17g/m^2 (4.5 oz/yd^2 ± 0.5 oz/yd^2) 100% cotton jersey knit underwear briefs and short-sleeve crew-neck tee shirts before the garment specimen is placed on the mannequin.

(5) Three specimens shall be tested.

6.21.2   Interpretation

6.21.2.1   One or more specimens failing this test shall constitute failing performance.

6.22   Chemical Permeation Resistance Test

6.22.1   Application

6.22.1.1   This method shall apply to LERL-1, LERL-2, LERL-3 and LERL-4 garment, visor, hand protection element and foot protection element materials and seams.

6.22.2   Samples and Specimens

6.22.2.1   Sample preparation prior to testing shall be as specified in Section 6.3.

6.22.2.2   Where the flexing and abrading conditioning is required in this section, all layers of composites shall be present and intact during the required conditioning.

6.22.2.3   A minimum of six specimens of each material and seam shall be tested against each chemical.

6.22.2.4   For composite materials, only the CBRN barrier material shall be tested for chemical permeation resistance.

6.22.3 **Test Procedure**

6.22.3.1 Samples shall be conditioned at a temperature of 32°C ± 3°C (90°F ± 5°F) and a relative humidity of 80 % ± 5 % for at least 24 hours immediately prior to permeation testing.

6.22.3.2 Specimens shall be tested for permeation resistance for 60 minutes +1 minute, -0 minutes against the chemicals specified in Sections 6.22.3.3 and 6.22.3.4 in accordance with ASTM Standard F739 with the following modifications:

(1) The test cells shall be designed to accommodate the introduction of liquid chemicals in a safe manner.

(2) The testing mode shall be open loop and the collection media shall be filtered air at a temperature of 32°C ± 3°C (90°F ± 5°F) and a relative humidity of 80% ± 5%, flowed through the collection chamber of the test cell at a rate of 1 Lpm ± 0.1 Lpm.

(3) The total amount of permeating chemical over a 60-minute period following initial contact of the material with the challenge chemical shall be determined.

(4) The cumulative permeation in micrograms per square centimeter at 60 minutes, +1 minute, –0 minutes of chemical exposure shall be determined.

(5) The selected method of detection shall have a sensitivity that is at least one order of magnitude less than the specified end point for the respective chemical over the 60-minute test period. The actual sensitivity of the selected method of detection shall be determined.

6.22.3.3 The following liquid chemicals shall be tested with the liquid concentration density specified in Table 6:

(1) Liquid chemical warfare agents.
   (a) HD; bis (2-chloroethyl) sulfide, CAS[16] 505-60-2; at 32°C ± 1°C (90°F ± 2°F).
   (b) GD; o-pinacolyl methylphosphonofluoridate, CAS 96-64-0; at 32°C ± 1°C (90°F ± 2°F).

(2) Liquid toxic industrial chemicals.
   (a) Acrolein (allyl aldehyde), CAS 107-02-8; at 32°C ± 1°C (90°F ± 2°F).
   (b) Acrylonitrile (VCN, cyanoethylene), CAS 107-13-1; at 32°C ±1°C (90°F ± 2°F).
   (c) Dimethyl sulfate (DMS, sulfuric acid dimethyl ester), CAS 77-78-1; at 32°C ± 1°C (90°F ± 2°F).

6.22.3.4 The following gases shall be tested with the concentration specified in Table 7:

(1) Ammonia, CAS 7664-41-7; at 32°C ± 1°C (90°F ± 2°F).

(2) Chlorine, Cl2; CAS 7782-50-5; at 32°C ± 1°C (90°F ± 2°F).

---

[16] CAS is an abbreviation for Chemical Abstracts Service, which is a division of the American Chemical Society.

Table 6. Liquid Concentration Densities

LERL	Liquid Concentration Density (g/m^2)
1	10 +1, -0
2	10 +1, -0
3	10 +1, -0
4	10 +1, -0

Table 7. Gas Concentrations

LERL	TIC	Gas Concentration (ppm)
1	Ammonia	1,000,000 +0, -50,000
1	Chlorine	1,000,000 +0, -50,000
2	Ammonia	1,000,000 +0, -50,000
2	Chlorine	1,000,000 +0, -50,000
3	Ammonia	900 +90, -0
3	Chlorine	30 +3, -0
4	Ammonia	900 +90, -0
4	Chlorine	30 +3, -0

6.22.3.5   For the liquid chemical warfare agents, the liquid drops shall be applied as nominal 1 μL drops uniformly distributed over the test area of the specimen surface. Where a seam or closure is included, at least one drop shall be applied to each critical juncture, such as the seam edge. The test cell shall be assembled in the closed-top configuration.

6.22.3.6   For gases, the cell assembly shall be in the closed-top configuration.

6.22.3.7   For the liquid toxic industrial chemicals, the test cell shall be assembled in the open-top configuration with 0.3 Lpm ± 0.03 Lpm of filtered air controlled at 80 % ± 5 %, relative humidity (RH) flowing through the top of the cell. With the open-top configuration, the test cell washer shall be allowed to be sealed by an impermeable nonreactive sealant.

6.22.4   **Report**

6.22.4.1   For permeation testing of chemical warfare agents and industrial chemicals the cumulative permeation in one hour shall be recorded and reported in μg/cm^2 for each specimen. The report shall include the pass or fail results for each chemical tested.

6.22.4.2   If no challenge chemical is detected at the end of the 60-minute test period, the cumulative permeation shall be reported as less than the minimum detectable mass per unit area for the specific chemical being tested.

6.22.4.3   The cumulative permeation shall be calculated for each specimen.

6.23   **LERL-1 Toxic Industrial Chemical Permeation Resistance Test**

6.23.1   **Application**

6.23.1.1 This method shall apply to LERL-1 garment, visor, hand protection element and foot protection element materials and seams.

6.23.1.2 Specimens shall be tested in accordance with NFPA 1991 Section 8.6 with the following modifications:

(1) Six material specimens shall be tested per chemical.

(2) Six specimens for each seam type shall be tested per chemical.

(3) Sample preparation prior to testing shall be as specified in Section 6.3.

(4) The challenge chemical shall be applied to the side of the specimen corresponding to the exterior surface of the ensemble element.

(5) Liquid toxic industrial chemicals (reagent grade) to be utilized during testing are as follows:[D]

- Acetone (2-propanone), CAS 67-64-1.
- Acetonitrile (cyanomethane), CAS 75-05-8.
- Carbon disulfide, CAS 75-15-0.
- Dichloromethane (methylene chloride), CAS 75-09-2.
- Diethylamine, CAS 109-89-7.
- Dimethylformamide (DMF), CAS 68-12-2.
- Ethyl acetate, CAS 141-78-6.
- n-Hexane, CAS 110-54-3.
- Methanol (methyl alcohol, carbinol), CAS 67-56-1.
- Nitrobenzene, CAS 98-95-3.
- Sodium hydroxide (50% w/w), CAS 1310-73-2.
- Sulfuric acid (93.1% sp gr 1.84, 66° Be8), CAS 7664-93-9.
- Tetrachloroethylene (perchloroethylene), CAS 127-18-4.
- Tetrahydrofuran (THF, 1,4-epoxybutane), CAS 109-99-9.
- Toluene (toluol), CAS 108-88-3.

(6) The following gases shall be tested with the concentration specified in Table 8:

- 1,3-Butadiene, inhibited, (99.0%), (bivinyl, vinylethylene, biethylene), CAS 106-99-0].
- Ethylene oxide, (99.7%), (oxirane, 1,2-epoxyethane), CAS 75-21-8.
- Hydrogen chloride, (99.0%), (hydrochloric acid), CAS 7647-01-0.
- Methyl chloride, (99.5%), (chloromethane), CAS 74-87-3.

Table 8. Gas Concentrations for LERL-1 Chemical Permeation Resistance Test

TIC	Gas Concentration (ppm)
1,3-Butadiene	1,000,000 +0, -50,000
Ethylene oxide	1,000,000 +0, -50,000
Hydrogen chloride	1,000,000 +0, -50,000
Methyl chloride	1,000,000 +0, -50,000

6.24   Viral Penetration Resistance Test

6.24.1   Application

6.24.1.1   This method shall apply to LERL-1, LERL-2, LERL-3 and LERL-4 garment, visor, hand protection element and foot protection element materials and seams.

6.24.1.2   Specimens shall be tested in accordance with ASTM Standard F1671 with the following modifications:

> (1) Sample preparation prior to testing shall be as specified in Section 6.3 with the following exception: The requirement to treat each test specimen with Break-Free® CLP® gun lubricant and synthetic sweat as specified in TOP-8-2-501, Appendix D shall be omitted.

> (2) Specimen exposure Procedure B shall be used.

> (3) Six material specimens shall be tested.

> (4) Six specimens of each seam type shall be tested.

> (5) The challenge chemical shall be applied to the side of the specimen corresponding to the exterior surface of the ensemble element.

6.25   Expulsion Test

6.25.1   Application

6.25.1.1   This method shall apply to LERL-1, LERL-2, LERL-3 and LERL-4 garment, visor, hand protection element and foot protection element materials and seams.

6.25.1.2   Specimens shall be tested as specified in TOP 8-2-501, Appendix C, Section 6.2, with the following modifications:

> (1) Sample preparation prior to testing shall be as specified in Section 6.3.

> (2) Six material specimens shall be tested.

> (3) Six specimens of each seam type shall be tested.

> (4) The challenge chemical shall be MeS.

> (5) The challenge chemical shall be applied to the side of the specimen corresponding to the exterior surface of the ensemble element.

6.26   **Rain Cabinet Test**

6.26.1   **Application**

6.26.1.1   This method shall apply to LERL-1, LERL-2, LERL-3 and LERL-4 garment, visor, hand protection element and foot protection element materials and seams.

6.26.1.2   Specimens shall be tested as specified in TOP 8-2-501, Section 4.3.7, with the following modifications:

(1) Sample preparation prior to testing shall be as specified in Section 6.3, with the exception that gun lubricant and synthetic sweat shall not be applied.

(2) Six material specimens shall be tested.

(3) Six specimens of each seam type shall be tested.

(4) The challenge chemical shall be TEP simulant.

(5) The duration of the rain exposure shall be a continuous one-hour cycle.

(6) The qualitative procedure shall be used.

(7) The challenge chemical shall be applied to the side of the specimen corresponding to the exterior surface of the ensemble element.

6.27   **Tearing Strength Test**

6.27.1   **Application**

6.27.2   This method shall apply to LERL-1, LERL-2, LERL-3 and LERL-4 woven garment and woven hand protection element materials.

6.27.3   ASTM Standard D1424 shall be applied with the following modifications:

(1) Samples shall be conditioned in accordance with the room temperature conditioning protocol (see Section 6.2.1) prior to testing.

(2) This test method shall apply to the woven outermost layer of all garment and hand protection element materials.

(3) Specimen Condition 1: Standard Testing Conditioning shall be used.

6.28   **Cold Temperature Performance Test**

6.28.1   **Application**

6.28.1.1   This method shall apply to LERL-1, LERL-2, LERL-3 and LERL-4 garment, hand protection element and foot protection element materials.

6.28.1.2   ASTM Standard D2136 shall be applied with the following modifications:

(1) Exposure temperature shall be -25°C (-13°F).

(2) Samples shall be conditioned in accordance with the room temperature conditioning protocol (see Section 6.2.1) prior to testing.

6.29   Burst Strength Test

6.29.1   Application

6.29.2   This method shall apply to LERL-1, LERL-2, LERL-3 and LERL-4 nonwoven garment and nonwoven hand protection element materials.

6.29.3   Samples shall be conditioned in accordance with the room temperature conditioning protocol (see Section 6.2.1) prior to testing.

6.29.4   Specimens shall be tested in accordance with ASTM Standard D3787.

6.29.4.1   This test method shall apply to the nonwoven outermost layer of all garment and hand protection element materials.

6.30   Seam/Closure Breaking Strength Test

6.30.1   Application

6.30.1.1   This method shall apply to LERL-1, LERL-2, LERL-3 and LERL-4 ensemble elements.

6.30.1.2   Specimens shall be tested in accordance with ASTM Standard D1683 with the following modifications:

(1) Samples shall be conditioned in accordance with the room temperature conditioning protocol (see Section 6.2.1) prior to testing.

(2) All specimens shall be taken from garment samples.

(3) Specimens shall include each type of seam and each type of closure.

6.30.1.3   The procedure for *Test Specimens from Manufactured Items,* ASTM Standard D1683, Section 7.4, shall be used for testing. Seam strength shall be determined.

6.31   Cut Resistance Test

6.31.1   Application

6.31.1.1   This method shall apply to LERL-1, LERL-2, LERL-3 and LERL-4 ensemble elements.

6.31.1.2   Specimens shall be tested in accordance with ASTM Standard F1790 with the following modifications:

(1) Samples shall be conditioned in accordance with the room temperature conditioning protocol (see Section 6.2.1) prior to testing.

(2) Five specimens in each of the warp and fill directions shall be tested.

6.31.1.3 For garment materials, if the garment element is constructed as a composite, the specimens shall consist of the composite.

6.31.1.4 For hand protection element materials, if the hand protection element is constructed as a composite, the specimens shall consist of the composite.

6.31.1.5 For foot protection element materials, if the foot protection element is constructed as a composite, the specimens shall consist of the composite. Specimens shall be taken from the thinnest part of the foot protection element.

6.32 **Puncture Resistance Test**

6.32.1 **Application**

6.32.1.1 This method shall apply to LERL-1, LERL-2, LERL-3 and LERL-4 ensemble elements.

6.32.1.2 Specimens shall be tested in accordance with ASTM Standard F1342 with the following modifications:

(1) Test Method A shall be used.

(2) Samples shall be conditioned in accordance with the room temperature conditioning protocol (see Section 6.2.1) prior to testing.

6.32.1.3 For garment materials, if the garment element is constructed as a composite, the specimens shall consist of the composite.

6.32.1.4 For hand protection element materials, if the hand protection element is constructed as a composite, the specimens shall consist of the composite.

6.32.1.5 For foot protection element materials, if the foot protection element is constructed as a composite, the specimens shall consist of the composite. Specimens shall be taken from the thinnest part of the foot protection element.

6.33 **Audible Signature Test**

6.33.1 **Application**

6.33.1.1 This test shall apply to LERL-1, LERL-2, LERL-3 and LERL-4 ensembles.

6.33.2 **Samples**

6.33.2.1 Four complete ensembles, without respiratory protection, are required as samples, consisting of two different sizes each for men and women. Samples shall be provided to fit, or to be adjustable to fit, the test subjects in accordance with the ensemble manufacturer's sizing provisions specific to each ensemble.

6.33.2.2   Samples shall be conditioned in accordance with the room temperature conditioning protocol (see Section 6.2.1) prior to testing.

6.33.3   Site Specifications

6.33.3.1   Testing shall be conducted in a hemi-anechoic room that is compatible with sound pressure measurement. The hemi-anechoic room shall be large enough to accommodate a 10-ft by 10-ft anechoic field, with the subject performing an exercise protocol within a 5-ft by 5-ft anechoic field. The hemi-anechoic room shall have a smooth concrete floor or equivalent. There shall be a communication system between the hemi-anechoic room and the control room for communication between the test subject and the test administrators.

6.33.3.2   The instrumentation system, including the microphone and cable, shall meet the requirements for a Type 1 instrument specified in IEC 61672-1. A 16-second data acquisition period shall be used.

6.33.3.3   The microphone shall be positioned at a height of 4 ft and a distance of 10 ft from the center of the 5-ft by 5-ft anechoic field such that microphone is to the right side of the test subject while the exercise motions are performed.

6.33.4   Procedure

6.33.4.1   The following sequence is to be performed by each subject wearing a tactical uniform and the ensemble.

6.33.4.2   The subject shall not wear a belt, law enforcement-specific equipment or personal jewelry.

6.33.4.3   The ensemble shall be donned in accordance with the ensemble manufacturer's instructions with the following exceptions:

- Respiratory protection shall not be worn.
- If the ensemble is encapsulating, head closures shall be left open a maximum of 6 in to permit the test subject to breathe during testing.

6.33.4.4   Sound pressure measurements shall be recorded while the subject performs the following protocol:

6.33.4.4.1 From a standing position, the subject shall drop to both knees, then drop down to stomach and crawl 3 ft with elbows, stomach and knees touching the floor. The subject shall then return to a standing position.

6.33.4.5   The elapsed exercise motion time shall be equal to or greater than 16 seconds and shall coincide with the 16-second data acquisition period.

6.33.4.6   Sound pressure measurements shall be measured in accordance with Section 6.33.4.4 once for each individual sample.

6.33.5 **Report**

6.33.5.1 The individual peak sound pressure level shall be recorded and reported for each test.

6.33.5.2 The average peak sound pressure level shall be calculated and reported for each ensemble. Refer to Annex A for details on the audible signature measurements and calculations. This average is to be reported as the audible signature.

6.33.6 **Interpretation**

6.33.6.1 The audible signature for the ensemble will be used as the pass/fail criterion.

6.34 **Total Heat Loss Test**

6.34.1 **Application**

6.34.2 This test shall apply to LERL-1, LERL-2, LERL-3 and LERL-4 garments.

6.34.3 ASTM Standard F1868 shall be applied with the following modifications:

(1) Part C shall be used.

(2) Samples shall be conditioned in accordance with the room temperature conditioning protocol (see Section 6.2.1) prior to testing.

(3) Six specimens of the garment composite shall be tested. The specimens shall not include areas of reinforcement, seams or closures, labels, etc.

6.35 **Thermal Protective Performance Test**

6.35.1 **Application**

6.35.1.1 This method shall apply to LERL-1 garment, hand protection element and foot protection element materials and seams.

6.35.1.2 Specimens shall be tested in accordance with Section 8.2 of NFPA 2112 with the following modifications:

(1) Samples shall be conditioned in accordance with the room temperature conditioning protocol (see Section 6.2.1) prior to testing.

(2) Six specimens shall be tested.

(3) Specimens shall not be laundered prior to testing.

(4) Testing shall be done only in the configuration using the spacer.

6.36   **Glove Hand Function Test**

6.36.1   **Application**

6.36.1.1   This test shall apply to LERL-1, LERL-2, LERL-3 and LERL-4 hand protection elements.

6.36.1.2   This test may be performed prior to the tactical or perimeter scenario test.

6.36.2   **Specimens**

6.36.2.1   Four pairs of hand protection elements are required as samples for testing.

6.36.2.2   Samples shall be sized to fit the test subjects, which include two males and two females.

6.36.2.3   Samples shall be conditioned in accordance with the ensemble conditioning protocol (see Section 6.2.1.1) prior to testing.

6.36.2.4   Subjects shall be in the complete ensemble, including respiratory protection.

6.36.3   **Apparatus**

6.36.3.1   The Complete Minnesota Dexterity Test apparatus (CMDT #32023A) shall be used.

6.36.3.2   Timing device.

6.36.4   **Procedure**

6.36.4.1   The turning test shall be used as modified below.

6.36.4.2   The following sequence is to be performed by each subject first while wearing a duty uniform to establish the baseline time and then while wearing the complete ensemble over the duty uniform. The test subject shall not be wearing hand protection elements for the baseline test.

6.36.4.3   The test apparatus shall be set up as follows: Place the first board on the table 1 in from the edge. Insert the disks into the holes in the board with the red side facing up. Place the other board directly to the left of the first board with the edges of the two boards even and in contact with each other. The boards shall be centered in front of the seated subject.

6.36.4.4   At a prompt from the timekeeper, the subject shall pick up a disk with his preferred hand from the upper corner on the preferred-hand side of the board. The subject shall turn the disk so the black side is up while passing it to the other hand and placing it in the corresponding position of the second board.

6.36.4.5   The subject shall continue working from preferred hand to non-preferred hand for each of the rows until all disks have been turned and positioned on the second board.

6.36.4.6   The timekeeper shall measure the timing to the nearest second. Timing shall commence when the subject touches the first disk and end when the last disk is placed in the second board.

6.36.4.6.1   The ensemble shall be examined for any visual breach of integrity prior to doffing.

6.36.4.6.2   The test subject shall doff the ensemble. Following doffing, the ensemble shall be examined for any visual breach of integrity.

6.36.5   **Calculation**

6.36.5.1   The percent degradation shall be calculated using Equation 4:

Equation 4. Percent Degradation for Glove Hand Function Test

$$X = \frac{Te - Tb}{Tb} \times 1\ 0$$

Where:
X = Percent degradation.
Tb = Baseline time (seconds) while wearing duty uniform.
Te = Time (seconds) while wearing ensemble.

6.36.5.2   Percent degradation shall be determined for each test.

6.36.6   **Report**

6.36.6.1   The baseline time (Tb) shall be recorded and reported for each subject.

6.36.6.2   The ensemble time (Te) shall be recorded and reported for each subject wearing an ensemble.

6.36.6.3   The percent degradation (X) shall be calculated and reported for each ensemble.

6.36.6.4   The average percent degradation (average of X) of all ensembles tested shall be calculated and reported.

6.36.6.5   Any visible breach of integrity of the ensemble prior to doffing shall be reported.

6.36.6.6   Any visible breach of integrity of the ensemble following doffing shall be reported.

6.36.7   **Interpretation**

6.36.7.1   The average percent degradation (average of X) of all ensembles tested shall be used as the pass/fail criterion.

6.36.7.2   Any visible breach of integrity of the ensemble prior to doffing shall constitute failing results.

6.36.7.3 Any visible breach of integrity of the ensemble following doffing shall constitute failing results.

6.37   **Fine Finger Dexterity Test**

6.37.1   **Application**

6.37.1.1 This test shall apply to LERL-1, LERL-2, LERL-3 and LERL-4 hand protection elements.

6.37.1.2 This test may be performed prior to the tactical or perimeter scenario test.

6.37.2   **Specimens**

6.37.2.1 Four pairs of hand protection elements are required as samples for testing.

6.37.2.2 Samples shall be sized to fit the test subjects, which include two males and two females.

6.37.2.3 Samples shall be conditioned in accordance with the ensemble conditioning protocol (see Section 6.2.1.1) prior to testing.

6.37.2.4 Subjects shall be in the complete ensemble, including respiratory protection.

6.37.3   **Apparatus**

6.37.3.1 The O'Connor Finger Dexterity Test apparatus shall be used. The apparatus consists of a board with 20 holes, each 3/16 in in diameter, a minimum of 60 pins, each 1 in long by 1/16 in in diameter and a dished area near the holes for pin storage.

6.37.3.2 Timing device.

6.37.4   **Procedure**

6.37.4.1 The following sequence is to be performed by each subject, first while wearing a duty uniform to establish the baseline time and then while wearing the complete ensemble over the duty uniform. The test subject shall not be wearing hand protection elements for the baseline test.

6.37.4.2 The subject shall pick up and place three pins in each of the 20 holes, using only the preferred hand and moving as quickly as possible.

6.37.4.3 Timing shall commence when the subject's hand touches the first pin. Timing shall cease when the subject completes the proper placement of the 60th pin.

6.37.4.4 The timekeeper shall measure the timing to the nearest second.

6.37.4.4.1 The ensemble shall be examined for any visual breach of integrity prior to doffing.

6.37.4.4.2 The test subject shall doff the ensemble. Following doffing, the ensemble shall be examined for any visual breach of integrity.

6.37.5   Calculation

6.37.5.1 The percent degradation shall be calculated using Equation 5:

Equation 5. Percent Degradation for Fine Finger Test

$$X = \frac{Te - Tb}{Tb} \times 1 \cdot 0$$

Where:
X = Percent degradation.
Tb = Baseline time (seconds) while wearing duty uniform.
Te = Time (seconds) while wearing ensemble.

6.37.5.2 Percent degradation shall be determined for each test.

6.37.6   Report

6.37.6.1 The baseline time (Tb) shall be recorded and reported for each subject.

6.37.6.2 The ensemble time (Te) shall be recorded and reported for each subject wearing an ensemble.

6.37.6.3 The percent degradation (X) shall be calculated and reported for each ensemble.

6.37.6.4 The average percent degradation (average of X) of all ensembles shall be calculated and reported.

6.37.6.5 Any visible breach of integrity of the ensemble prior to doffing shall be reported.

6.37.6.6 Any visible breach of integrity of the ensemble following doffing shall be reported.

6.37.7   Interpretation

6.37.7.1 The average percent degradation (average of X) of all ensembles tested shall be used as the pass/fail criterion.

6.37.7.2 Any visible breach of integrity of the ensemble prior to doffing shall constitute failing results.

6.37.7.3 Any visible breach of integrity of the ensemble following doffing shall constitute failing results.

6.38   **Grip Test**

6.38.1   Application

6.38.1.1 This method shall be applied to LERL-1, LERL-2, LERL-3 and LERL-4 hand protection elements.

6.38.1.2 Hand protection element specimens shall be tested in accordance with NFPA 1951, Section 8.29, with the following modifications:

(1) Five pairs each in both the largest and smallest sizes shall be conditioned as specified in NFPA 1951, Section 8.1.2.

(2) Five pairs each in both the largest and smallest sizes shall be conditioned as specified in NFPA 1951, Section 8.1.2, followed by conditioning as specified in NFPA 1951, Section 8.1.7.

6.39   **Abrasion Resistance Test**

6.39.1   **Application**

6.39.1.1 This method shall apply to LERL-1, LERL-2, LERL-3 and LERL-4 foot protection element materials.

6.39.1.2 Specimens shall be tested in accordance with ASTM Standard D1630 with the following modifications:

(1) Samples shall be conditioned in accordance with the room temperature conditioning protocol (see Section 6.2.1) prior to testing.

(2) Ten specimens (from ensemble foot protection element) shall be tested.

6.40   **Flame Resistance Test**

6.40.1   **Application**

6.40.1.1 This method shall apply to LERL-1 garment, hand protection element and foot protection element materials and seams.

6.40.1.2 Specimens shall be tested in accordance with ASTM Standard D6413 with the following modifications:

(1) Samples shall be conditioned in accordance with the room temperature conditioning protocol (see Section 6.2.1) prior to testing.

(2) Ten specimens (from an ensemble) in each of the warp and fill directions shall be tested.

6.41   Overall Liquid Integrity Test

6.41.1   Application

6.41.1.1   This test method shall apply to LERL-1, LERL-2, LERL-3 and LERL-4 ensembles.

6.41.1.2   Samples shall be conditioned in accordance with the Room Temperature Conditioning Protocol (see Section 6.2.1) prior to testing.

6.41.2   Specimens shall be tested in accordance with ASTM Standard F1359 with the following modifications:

(1) Six specimens shall be tested with each model of respiratory protection specified by the ensemble manufacturer for use with that ensemble model.

(2) Exposure periods shall be as specified below:
- LERL-1:   Eight min.
- LERL-2:   Eight min.
- LERL-3:   Four min.
- LERL-4:   Two min.

(3) Fluorescent or colored dyes shall not be added to the water.

(4) The liquid-absorptive garment shall cover all portions of the mannequin that are covered by the test specimen.

(5) The specimen shall be inspected within 10 min of the end of the liquid spray exposure period for evidence of liquid penetration.

6.42   Slip Resistance Test

6.42.1   Application

6.42.1.1   This test method shall apply to LERL-1, LERL-2, LERL-3 and LERL-4 footwear and footwear cover soles.

6.42.2   Specimens

6.42.2.1   Samples shall be conditioned in accordance with the room temperature conditioning protocol (see Section 6.2.1) prior to testing.

6.42.2.2   A minimum of three footwear specimens or footwear cover specimens (as applicable) shall be tested.

6.42.3   Procedure

6.42.3.1   Slip resistance shall be performed in accordance with ASTM Standard F489 in a dry and a wet condition, with wet conditioning performed by pouring distilled or deionized water on the reference tile prior to each test.

6.42.4   Report

6.42.4.1 The static coefficient of friction of each specimen shall be recorded and reported.

6.42.5   Interpretation

6.42.5.1 One or more specimens failing this test shall constitute failing performance.

6.43   Field of View Test

6.43.1   Application

6.43.1.1 This test shall apply to garments containing a visor. The VFS shall be obtained by using a medium-size or equivalent respiratory protection sized to fit the head form described in EN 136, Figure 14 or equivalent. The garment hood or portion covering the head shall be positioned over the respiratory protection.

6.43.1.2 Each model of respiratory protection specified by the ensemble manufacturer for use with each ensemble model shall be tested.

6.43.1.3 Samples shall be conditioned in accordance with the room temperature conditioning protocol (see Section 6.2.1) prior to testing.

6.43.1.4 The VFS is determined by using a VFS grid (dots on visual field) as defined in the *American Medical Association Guides to the Evaluation of Permanent Impairment, 5th Edition* that is overlaid on the diagram of the visual field plot obtained using the spherical shell of the EN 136 apertometer or equivalent.

6.43.1.5 The VFS is the average of three fittings of the same garment and respiratory protection on the specified head form.

6.43.2   Report

6.43.2.1 The VFS for each respiratory protection fitting shall be recorded and reported.

6.43.2.2 The average VFS for all respiratory protection fittings shall be recorded and reported.

6.43.3   Interpretation

6.43.3.1 The average VFS is used as the pass/fail criterion.

6.44   Color/Visibility Test Method

6.44.1   Application

6.44.1.1 This test shall apply to LERL-1, LERL-2, LERL-3 and LERL-4 garment, hand protection element and foot protection element outer materials.

6.44.2   **Specimens**

6.44.2.1   Samples shall be conditioned in accordance with the room temperature conditioning protocol (see Section 6.2.1) prior to testing.

6.44.2.2   A minimum of three specimens shall be tested for each distinct color present on the garment, hand protection elements and foot protection element outer materials.

6.44.3   **Procedure**

6.44.3.1   Specimens shall be measured using a color measurement spectrophotometer.

6.44.3.2   The spectrophotometer shall be configured as follows:

(1) Color Scale: CIE L*, a*, b*.

(2) CIE Illuminant: D65.

(3) CIE Standard Observer: 10°.

(4) Instrument Geometry: 45°/0° or 0°/45°.

6.44.3.3   Samples shall be measured on the spectrophotometer according to AATCC Evaluation Procedure 6: Instrumental Color Measurement.

6.44.4   **Report**

6.44.4.1   Measured L* and Y brightness values shall be recorded and reported for each test.

7. LABELING AND INFORMATION

7.1 General Product Label Requirements for CBRN Protective Ensemble Models[17]

7.1.1 For ensembles having garments with attached hand protection and foot protection elements, each ensemble shall have an ensemble product label permanently attached to, embossed on or printed on the inside of the garment element (including each piece of a multipiece integrated garment). Attached hand protection and foot protection elements are not required to have individual product labels.

7.1.2 For ensembles having garments intended for use with detached hand protection and foot protection elements, each ensemble shall have an ensemble product label permanently attached to, embossed on or printed on the inside of the garment element (including each piece of a multipiece integrated garment).

7.1.3 Each detached hand protection element or element type shall have a product label permanently attached to, embossed on or printed on the top inside of the gauntlet (i.e., wrist/arm portion) of each element or element type.

7.1.4 Each detached foot protection element or element type shall have a product label permanently attached to, embossed on or printed on the inside of each element or element type.

7.1.5 Multiple label pieces may be used in order to carry all statements and information required on a product label; however, all label pieces composing an entire product label shall be located adjacent to each other. [A]

7.1.6 All worded portions of a required product label shall appear in English. Other languages may be added. [A]

7.1.7 Symbols and other pictorial graphic representations may be used to supplement worded statements on product labels, provided such symbols and other pictorial graphic representations are clearly explained in the user information. [A]

7.1.8 For each compliant ensemble model, each ensemble product label shall include the compliance and information statements specified in Sections 7.2 and 7.3 as applicable to the ensemble.

7.1.9 In addition to the compliance and information statements required by Section 7.1.8, at least the following information shall be printed legibly on the ensemble product label in letters at least 3.2 mm (1/8 in) high: [A]

- Legal name and legal address of the ensemble manufacturer.

- Address of manufacturing location (city, state/province, country).

- Date of manufacture (i.e., month and year).

---

[17] Refer to Annex D, Table 10 and Table 11 for a brief summary as to the placement of labeling and information on or with the ensemble and its elements.

- Ensemble model number.
  - If the ensemble model has detached hand or foot protection elements, the ensemble product label shall include the detached element or element type model numbers for the elements or element types that must be used in order for the ensemble model to be compliant.

- Serial number for the ensemble.

- Size.

- Visor material(s), if any.

- Respiratory protection model(s) that must be used in order for the ensemble model to be compliant.

- Garment, attached hand protection element and attached foot protection element material(s) as applicable.
  - All listings of materials shall specify either the generic material names or trade names if the composition of the material is proprietary.

7.1.10 In addition to the compliance and information statements required by Section 7.1.8, detached hand or foot protection ensemble elements or element types shall have at least the following information printed legibly on the product label(s) in letters at least 3.2 mm (1/8 in) high: [A]

- Legal name of the ensemble manufacturer.

- Date of manufacture (i.e., month and year).

- Ensemble element or element type model number.

- Size.

- Ensemble element or element type material(s), as applicable.
  - All listings of materials shall specify either the generic material names or trade names if the composition of the material is proprietary.

7.2 **Compliance Statements on Ensemble Product Labels of Compliant Ensemble Models**

7.2.1 Placement of any compliance statement on the ensemble product label shall be consistent with Sections 7.1.1 and 7.1.2.

7.2.2 An ensemble of a compliant ensemble model shall have the following compliance statement on the ensemble product label in letters at least 2.5 mm (3/32 in) high. The label shall indicate the associated LERL and whether the ensemble model is encapsulating or nonencapsulating.

"PURSUANT TO NIJ CR-0116.00, THIS [*insert* LERL-1, LERL-2, LERL-3 *or* LERL-4 *here*] [*insert* ENCAPSULATING *or* NONENCAPSULATING *here*] CBRN PROTECTIVE ENSEMBLE MODEL HAS BEEN TESTED AND FOUND TO BE COMPLIANT WITH THE REQUIREMENTS OF NIJ STANDARD-0116.00

(CBRN PROTECTIVE ENSEMBLE STANDARD FOR LAW ENFORCEMENT) FOR THE ABOVE-NOTED LEVEL. DO NOT REMOVE THIS LABEL."

7.2.3 If the ensemble model is intended to be worn only once, the following statement shall be included with the language in Section 7.2.2:

"FOR SINGLE USE ONLY"

7.2.4 Following the text in Section 7.2.2, the following statement shall be made on the ensemble product label in letters at least 3.2 mm (1/8 in) high:

"The technical data package contains information on CBRN hazards against which this model is certified. Consult the technical data package and ensemble manufacturer's instructions before use."

7.3 **Limited Flash Fire Protection Statement on Compliant LERL-1 Ensemble Models**

7.3.1 Placement of the flash fire protection statement on the ensemble product label shall be consistent with Sections 7.1.1 and 7.1.2.

7.3.2 Each LERL-1 ensemble product label shall have the following statement in letters at least 2.5 mm (3/32 in) high.

"THIS LERL-1 CBRN PROTECTIVE ENSEMBLE MODEL OF WHICH THIS GARMENT ELEMENT IS A PART HAS BEEN TESTED AND MEETS THE (VERY LIMITED) FLASH FIRE PROTECTION PERFORMANCE REQUIREMENTS OF SECTION 5.1.2.16 of NIJ STANDARD-0116.00."

7.4 **User Information to Be Provided by the Ensemble Manufacturer**

7.4.1 In order to have an ensemble model tested under this standard, the ensemble manufacturer must agree that, if the model is found to be compliant, it will provide written user information including, but not limited to, warnings, information and instructions with each individual ensemble (and with each ensemble element, other than respiratory protection, that may be acquired or provided separately).

7.4.2 The ensemble manufacturer shall provide the required user information in such a manner as to make such information clear, prominent and immediately available to any user of the ensemble or ensemble elements.

7.4.3 The ensemble manufacturer shall provide at least the following warnings, information and instructions as part of the written user information: [A]

- Description of LERL: The text below shall be included as appropriate depending on the protection level of the compliant ensemble model:

  o LERL-1 CBRN protective ensembles are intended to provide limited protection to law enforcement personnel making tactical entry into environments involving CBRN hazards, conditions in which contaminant concentrations are unknown or are known to be at or above immediately dangerous to life and health (IDLH) levels requiring the use of a self-contained breathing apparatus (SCBA), and flame and flash fire hazards. LERL-1 ensembles are intended to withstand the rigorous use associated with tactical operations. These ensemble models are tested against two chemical warfare agents and 24 toxic industrial chemicals that are representative of many chemical threats.

o   LERL-2 CBRN protective ensembles are intended to provide limited protection to law enforcement personnel making tactical entry into environments involving CBRN hazards and conditions in which contaminant concentrations are unknown or are known to be at or above immediately dangerous to life and health (IDLH) levels requiring the use of a self-contained breathing apparatus (SCBA). LERL-2 ensembles are intended to withstand the rigorous use associated with tactical operations. These ensemble models are tested against two chemical warfare agents and five toxic industrial chemicals.

o   LERL-3 CBRN protective ensembles are intended to provide limited protection to law enforcement personnel making tactical entry into environments involving CBRN hazards and conditions in which contaminant concentrations are known to be below immediately dangerous to life and health (IDLH) levels permitting the use of an air purifying respirator (APR) or powered APR (PAPR). LERL-3 ensembles are intended to withstand the rigorous use associated with tactical operations. These ensemble models are tested against two chemical warfare agents and five toxic industrial chemicals.

o   LERL-4 CBRN protective ensembles are intended to provide limited protection to law enforcement personnel performing perimeter operations at incidents involving CBRN hazards and conditions in which contaminant concentrations are known to be below immediately dangerous to life and health (IDLH) levels permitting the use of an air purifying respirator (APR) or powered APR (PAPR) and where mission tasks require less stringent ensemble durability. These ensemble models are tested against two chemical warfare agents and five toxic industrial chemicals.

- Pre-use information as follows:
  o   Safety considerations.
  o   Recommendations and precautions regarding the application of law enforcement agency markings after purchase.
  o   Statement that most performance properties of the ensemble cannot be tested by the user in the field.
  o   Recommended type(s) of closure lubricant(s) as applicable.
  o   Recommended type(s) of anti-fog agents as applicable.
  o   Recommended anti-fog procedures as applicable.

- o Any limitations or precautions as to type(s) of clothing worn under the ensemble.
- o Warranty information including length of warranty.

- Donning and doffing information as follows:
  - o Donning and doffing procedures including ensemble interface considerations.
  - o Sizing and adjustment procedures.

- Recommended use in accordance with the following:
  - o For users in the United States, applicable provisions of 29 C.F.R. Part 1910, Subpart I.
  - o For users in other countries, a statement recommending that users consult any applicable law regarding CBRN protective equipment.

- Care and maintenance as follows:
  - o Cleaning instructions and precautions.
  - o Recommended decontamination procedures
  - o Recommended storage conditions and life expectancy when stored under those conditions.
  - o Inspection details.
  - o Repair methods where applicable.
  - o Retirement and disposal criteria and considerations.

- If the ensemble is intended for single exposure only, a statement shall be included that the ensemble is intended for single exposure only.

- Manufacturer and model(s) of specific respiratory protection successfully tested with the ensemble model.

7.5 Technical Data Package to Be Provided by the Ensemble Manufacturer

7.5.1 In order to have an ensemble model tested under this standard, the ensemble manufacturer must agree that, if the model is found to be compliant, it will furnish, as set forth in Section 7.6, a technical data package for the ensemble model upon the request of the purchaser or the prospective purchaser.

7.5.2 The technical data package shall contain all data showing compliance of the model with this standard. The $PPDF_i$ and $PPDF_{sys}$ for each ensemble model shall be included as part of the technical data package.

7.5.3 In the technical data package, the ensemble manufacturer shall describe the ensemble model (including its garment, hand protection and foot protection elements) in terms of the model number, replaceable components, available options, accessories, testing devices and available sizes. [A]

7.5.3.1 Descriptions of size shall include the ranges in height and weight for persons fitting each particular available size of garment.

7.5.3.2 Descriptions also shall provide information as to whether and how the sizes apply to persons wearing helmets (such as tactical ballistic helmets), communications devices and other similar equipment. [A]

7.5.4 The technical data package shall provide the following information for the respiratory protection successfully tested with the ensemble model.
- Manufacturer and specific model(s) of respiratory protection successfully tested with the ensemble model.
- Exhaust valve type(s) and material(s).
- External fitting type(s) and material(s).
- External gasket type(s) and material(s).

7.5.5 The technical data package shall include a list and descriptions of the following with respect to the ensemble model, as applicable:[A]

- All ensemble elements and components (other than respiratory protection):
  - Element and component materials (material compositions shall specify either the generic material names or trade names if the composition of the material is proprietary).
  - Element and component material seam types and composition.
  - Element and component methods of attachment.
  - Element closures:
    - Type(s) of closures.
    - Material(s) of construction for the closure, including zipper chain, slide, pull and tape.
    - Location and description of any closure assembly.
  - Visor: Permanent or detachable covers and films as applicable.
  - Garment element:
    - Type(s) of surface treatments, as applicable.
  - Hand protection elements:
    - Type(s) of interfaces.
    - Type(s) of linings or surface treatments as applicable.
    - Available hand protection element sizes and dimensional data for size determination.
  - Foot protection elements:
    - Type(s) of interfaces.
    - Type(s) of linings or surface treatments as applicable.
    - Type(s) of soles or special toe reinforcements.
    - Available foot protection element sizes.

ANNEX A. Acoustic Measurements and Calculations

Measurements
All measurements are one-third octave sound pressure level averages. The averaging time is 32 seconds with a single stationary microphone position for each source. The third octaves from 50 Hz to 10,000 Hz are used for the calculations.

Calculations
Take all of the sound pressure level measurements for each one-third octave and average them in the pressure domain. Use Equation 6 to convert all of the sound pressures levels (dB re: 20 uPa) to pressure levels in Pascals. L_{pt} is the sound pressure level in one-third octave bands. Use Equation 7 to average the pressure levels and convert them back to decibel levels. P_t is the pressure level in one-third octave bands. L_{Apt} is the average of the sound pressure levels in one-third octave bands.

Equation 6. Converting Sound Pressure to Pressure

$$P_t = 0.00002 \text{ Pa} \bullet 10^{(Lpt/10)}$$

Equation 7. Averaging Pressure and Converting to Sound Pressure

$$L_{Apt} = 10 * \log \frac{1}{n} \sum_{n=1}^{n} \frac{P_{tn}}{0.00002 \ Pa}$$

Where **n** is the number of sources.

The averaged sound pressure levels need to be corrected for background levels and checked to be sure that there was no contamination.

If the difference of the average and the background levels is between six and 10 decibels, use Equation 8 to correct the average sound pressure. Subtract the result of Equation 8 from the measured source sound pressure level as indicated in Equation 9.

If the difference of the average and the background levels is between two and six decibels, the background correction formula is still used but the data are marked with an asterisk to indicate contamination.

If the difference of the average and the background levels is less than two decibels, the data are marked with a double asterisk and the data are not corrected. The double asterisk indicates high levels of contamination. If any double asterisks are found then the background levels need to be lowered before testing can resume. L_{Bt} are the background levels in one-third octave bands. L_{AptB} are the average one-third octave sound pressure levels corrected for background.

Equation 8. Background Correction

$$Background\ Correction = -10 \log(1 - 10^{0.1*(L_{Apt} - L_{Bt})})$$

Equation 9. Background Corrected Sound Level

$$L_{AptB} = L_{Apt} - Background\,Correction$$

Next, apply the A-weighting values in Table 9 to the background corrected sound levels by adding the sound pressure level, L_{AptB}, for each one-third octave band to the corresponding values in Table 1 as indicated by Equation 10.

Table 9. A-Weighting Values

Frequency (Hz)	A (dB Correction)	Frequency (Hz)	A (dB Correction)	Frequency (Hz)	A (dB Correction)	Frequency (Hz)	A (dB Correction)
50	-30.2	200	-10.9	800	-0.8	3150	1.2
63	-26.2	250	-8.6	1000	0.0	4000	1.0
80	-22.5	315	-6.6	1250	0.6	5000	0.5
100	-19.1	400	-4.8	1600	1.0	6300	-0.1
125	-16.1	500	-3.2	2000	1.2	8000	-1.1
160	-13.4	630	-1.9	2500	1.3	10000	-2.5

Equation 10. A-Weighting Addition Formula

$$L_{AptBA} = L_{AptB} + A$$

where A = A-weighting values

The final step is summing the A-weighting corrected values to determine an overall A-weighted sound level as shown in Equation 11. L_{AptBA} are the averaged A-weighted sound pressure levels corrected for background in one-third octaves. L_{pAT} is the total A-weighted value. L_{pT} is the total sound pressure level.

Equation 11. Summation Formula

$$L_{pAT} = 10 \bullet \log \frac{1}{n} \sum_{n=1}^{n} 10^{0.1 * L_{AptBAn}}$$

Where **n** is the number of one-third octaves.

The sound pressure levels are referenced to 20 micro-Pascals.

ANNEX B. Summary Table of Conditioning Requirements[18]

Sample Preparation and Conditioning	Test Method
• Room Temperature Conditioning	ASTM Standard D1776, Samples must be tested within five minutes of removal from conditioning • 21°C ± 3°C, RH 65% ± 5% for 24 hours
• Hot Diurnal Environment Conditioning	MIL-STD-810F, Method 501.4; Table 501.4-II • Diurnal (repeating daily) cycle 35°C to 71°C; Duration of 504 hours (three weeks)
• Cold Constant Environmental Conditioning	MIL-STD-810F, Method 502.4, Basic Cold (C1) • Temperature: -32°C; Test duration of 72 hours (three days)
• Humidity Environmental Conditioning	MIL-STD-810E, Method 507.3; Table 507.3-II • Natural cycle, Cycle 1, Diurnal Cycle 31°C, RH 88% to 41°C, RH 59%; Duration of 120 hours (five days)
• Vibration Conditioning	MIL-STD-810F, Method 514.5; Conditions shall be U.S. Highway Vibration, Unrestrained, Figure 514.5C-1 • Duration of 12 hours/axis, three axes; Total duration of 36 hours
• Ensemble Conditioning	Sequence: • Hot Diurnal, Cold Constant Environmental Conditioning, Humidity Environmental Conditioning, Vibration Conditioning, Room Temperature Conditioning
• Swatch Conditioning	Sequence: • Hot Diurnal, Cold Constant Environmental Conditioning, Humidity Environmental Conditioning, Vibration Conditioning
• Sample Preparation	Garment materials: • Swatch conditioning protocol • ASTM Standard F392 with modifications • ASTM Standard D4157 with modifications, plus treatment with gun lube and synthetic sweat per TOP 8-2-501, Appendix D Hand protection elements materials: • Ensemble Conditioning protocol • Fine Finger Dexterity conditioning • Treatment with gun lube and synthetic sweat per TOP 8-2-501, Appendix D

---

[18] Please refer to the text of this NIJ standard (in particular, Chapter 6) for complete details. Should there be any discrepancy between that text and this summary annex, the former controls.

Sample Preparation and Conditioning	Test Method
	Foot protection upper materials: • Ensemble Conditioning protocol • FIA 1209 • ASTM Standard D4157 with modifications, plus treatment with gun lube and synthetic sweat per TOP 8-2-501, Appendix D Foot protection element sole materials: • Swatch Conditioning protocol • ASTM Standard D4157 with modifications, plus treatment with gun lube and synthetic sweat per TOP 8-2-501, Appendix D Seam sample preparation: • Swatch Conditioning protocol • Treatment with gun lube and synthetic sweat per TOP 8-2-501, Appendix D

ANNEX C. Summary Table of Requirements and Test Methods[19]

System Level Requirements (complete ensemble)

Requirement	Test Method	LERL-1	LERL-2	LERL-3	LERL-4
• Require SCBA or PAPR/APR		• Requires SCBA	• Requires SCBA	• Requires APR/PAPR	• Requires APR/PAPR
• System Level Chemical Vapor Protection	Test: Section 6.4, MIST • Applies ASTM Standard F2588, with NIJ modifications: (1) Ensemble Conditioning, (2) rest portion of ASTM Standard F2588, Section 12.3.5.9 replaced by "lying prone on floor, facing the wind and simulating a sighting and firing sequence for one minute," (3) Specimens: four ensembles (two different sizes for males; two different sizes for females)	• Average local $PPDF_i$ value at each PAD location for the four ensembles tested of no less than 360.0 • Systemic PPDF ($PPDF_{SYS}$) value for each tested ensemble of no less than 361.0	• Average local $PPDF_i$ value at each PAD location for the four ensembles tested of no less than 360.0 • Systemic PPDF ($PPDF_{SYS}$) value for each tested ensemble of no less than 361.0	• Average local $PPDF_i$ value at each PAD location for the four ensembles tested of no less than 120.0 • Systemic PPDF ($PPDF_{SYS}$) value for each tested ensemble of no less than 76.0	• Average local $PPDF_i$ value at each PAD location for the four ensembles tested of no less than 120.0 • Systemic PPDF ($PPDF_{SYS}$) value for each tested ensemble of no less than 76.0
• System Level Ergonomics Requirement	Test: Section 6.6, Donning and Doffing • Specimens: Four ensembles (two different sizes for males; two different sizes for females) • Conditioning: Ensemble Conditioning	• Average donning time of no greater than eight minutes • Average doffing time of no greater than three minutes • No visible breach of integrity	• Average donning time of no greater than eight minutes • Average doffing time of no greater than three minutes • No visible breach of integrity	• Average donning time of no greater than seven minutes • Average doffing time of no greater than three minutes • No visible breach of integrity	• Average donning time of no greater than seven minutes • Average doffing time of no greater than three minutes • No visible breach of integrity
• System Level Ergonomics Requirement	Test: Section 6.7, Gross Body Mobility Tests • Specimens: Four ensembles (two different sizes for males; two different sizes for females) • Conditioning: Ensemble Conditioning	Average of <10% degradation in distance covered or range of motion for the following: • Forward walking test • Backward walking test • Side step walking test • Upper arm abduction test	Average of <10% degradation in distance covered or range of motion for the following: • Forward walking test • Backward walking test • Side step walking test • Upper arm abduction test	Average of <10% degradation in distance covered or range of motion for the following: • Forward walking test • Backward walking test • Side step walking test • Upper arm abduction test	Average of <10% degradation in distance covered or range of motion for the following: • Forward walking test • Backward walking test • Side step walking test • Upper arm abduction test

---

[19] Please refer to the text of this NIJ standard (in particular, Chapter 6) for complete details. Should there be any discrepancy between that text and this summary annex, the former controls.

CBRN Protective Ensemble Standard for Law Enforcement

Requirement	Test Method	LERL-1	LERL-2	LERL-3	LERL-4
		• Upper arm forward extension test • Upper arm backward extension test • Upper leg forward extension test • Upper leg backward extension test • Standing trunk flexion test: average of <25% degradation in distance • Upper leg flexion: Average of <15% degradation in range of motion • Kneel and rise test: Shall kneel and rise with no assistance • No visible breach of integrity	• Upper arm forward extension test • Upper arm backward extension test • Upper leg forward extension test • Upper leg backward extension test • Standing trunk flexion test: average of <25% degradation in distance • Upper leg flexion: Average of <15% degradation in range of motion • Kneel and rise test: Shall kneel and rise with no assistance • No visible breach of integrity	• Upper arm forward extension test • Upper arm backward extension test • Upper leg forward extension test • Upper leg backward extension test • Standing trunk flexion test: average of <25% degradation in distance • Upper leg flexion: Average of <15% degradation in range of motion • Kneel and rise test: Shall kneel and rise with no assistance • No visible breach of integrity	• Upper arm forward extension test • Upper arm backward extension test • Upper leg forward extension test • Upper leg backward extension test • Standing trunk flexion test: average of <25% degradation in distance • Upper leg flexion: Average of <15% degradation in range of motion • Kneel and rise test: Shall kneel and rise with no assistance • No visible breach of integrity
• System Level Ergonomics Requirement	Test: Section 6.19, Tactical Scenario Test • Specimens: Four ensembles (two different sizes for males; two different sizes for females) Conditioning: Ensemble Conditioning	• Average % degradation in time of <20% • Completion of all tasks • No visible breach of integrity	• Average % degradation in time of <20% • Completion of all tasks • No visible breach of integrity	• Average % degradation in time of <20% • Completion of all tasks • No visible breach of integrity	• N/A
• System Level Ergonomics Requirement	Test: Section 6.20, Perimeter Scenario Test • Specimens: Four ensembles (two different sizes for males; two different sizes for females) Conditioning: Ensemble Conditioning	• N/A	• N/A	• N/A	• Average % degradation in time of <25% • Completion of all tasks • No visible breach of integrity

CBRN Protective Ensemble Standard for Law Enforcement

System Level Ergonomics Requirement	Test: Section 6.36, Glove Hand Function Test (Gross Dexterity) • Specimens: Four pairs of hand protection elements (two different sizes for males; two different sizes for females) • Conditioning: Ensemble Conditioning • Complete Minnesota Dexterity Test (CMDT#32023A) apparatus; subjects in full CBRN ensemble, including respiratory protection	• Overall % degradation over bare-handed manipulation of <35% • No visible breach of integrity	• Overall % degradation over bare-handed manipulation of <35% • No visible breach of integrity	• Overall % degradation over bare-handed manipulation of <35% • No visible breach of integrity	• Overall % degradation over bare-handed manipulation of <35% • No visible breach of integrity
System Level Ergonomics Requirement	Test: Section 6.37, Fine Finger Dexterity Test (Fine Dexterity) • Specimens: Four pairs of hand protection elements (two different sizes for males; two different sizes for females) • Conditioning: Ensemble Conditioning • O'Connor Fine Finger Dexterity Test; subjects in full CBRN ensemble, including respiratory protection	• Overall % degradation over bare-handed manipulation of <50% • No visible breach of integrity	• Overall % degradation over bare-handed manipulation of <50% • No visible breach of integrity	• Overall % degradation over bare-handed manipulation of <50% • No visible breach of integrity	• Overall % degradation over bare-handed manipulation of <50% • No visible breach of integrity
System Level Ergonomics Requirement	Test: Section 6.43, Field of View Test • Specimens: one garment hood or portion covering the head and containing a visor • Conditioning: Room Temperature Conditioning • Applies EN136 Method	VFS ≥ 90	VFS ≥ 90	VFS ≥ 90	VFS ≥ 90
System Level Overall Liquid Penetration Resistance	Test: Section 6.41, Overall Liquid Integrity Test • Specimens: Six complete ensembles • Conditioning: Room Temperature Conditioning • Applies ASTM Standard F1359 with NIJ modifications	• No liquid penetration following an eight-minute exposure	• No liquid penetration following an eight-minute exposure	• No liquid penetration following a four-minute exposure	• No liquid penetration following a two-minute exposure

• Notes: 　• Test does not simulate any particular end-use condition but rather evaluates the ability of the construction and configuration to resist liquid penetration 　• ASTM Standard F1359 specifies water spray from five nozzles for 15 minutes in each of four orientations (total time 60 minutes) – this NIJ standard modifies time requirements				
• **System Level Audible Signature**	Test: Section 6.33, Audible Signature Test • Specimens: Four ensembles without respirators (two different sizes for males; two different sizes for females) • Conditioning: Room Temperature Conditioning	• Audible signature of ≤ 55DBA	• Audible signature of ≤ 55DBA	• Audible signature of ≤ 45DBA	• Audible signature of ≤ 45DBA

CBRN Protective Ensemble Standard for Law Enforcement

Garment Level Requirements:

Requirement	Test Method	LERL-1	LERL-2	LERL-3	LERL-4
• Garment Level Chemical Permeation Resistance	Test: Section 6.22, Chemical Permeation Resistance Test • Specimens: Six swatches of each material and seam • Conditioning: Sample Preparation and conditioning at 32°C ± 3°C, RH 80% ± 5% for 24 hours immediately prior to testing • Applies ASTM Standard F739 with modifications	• HD: Cumulative permeation in one hour shall not exceed 4.0μg/cm^2 for each specimen tested • GD: Cumulative permeation in one hour shall not exceed 1.25μg/cm^2 for each specimen tested • For liquid and gaseous TICs listed below, cumulative permeation in one hour shall not exceed 6.0μg/cm^2 for each specimen tested (list from NFPA 1994): 1. Acrolein 2. Acrylonitrile 3. Dimethyl sulfate 4. Ammonia (gas) 5. Chlorine (gas)	• HD: Cumulative permeation in one hour shall not exceed 4.0μg/cm^2 for each specimen tested • GD: Cumulative permeation in one hour shall not exceed 1.25μg/cm^2 for each specimen tested • For liquid and gaseous TICs listed below, cumulative permeation in one hour shall not exceed 6.0μg/cm^2 for each specimen tested (list from NFPA 1994): 1. Acrolein 2. Acrylonitrile 3. Dimethyl sulfate 4. Ammonia (gas) 5. Chlorine (gas)	• HD: Cumulative permeation in one hour shall not exceed 4.0μg/cm^2 for each specimen tested • GD: Cumulative permeation in one hour shall not exceed 1.25μg/cm^2 for each specimen tested • For liquid and gaseous TICs listed below, cumulative permeation in one hour shall not exceed 6.0μg/cm^2 for each specimen tested (list from NFPA 1994): 1. Acrolein 2. Acrylonitrile 3. Dimethyl sulfate 4. Ammonia (gas) 5. Chlorine (gas)	• HD: Cumulative permeation in one hour shall not exceed 4.0μg/cm^2 for each specimen tested • GD: Cumulative permeation in one hour shall not exceed 1.25μg/cm^2 for each specimen tested • For liquid and gaseous TICs listed below, cumulative permeation in one hour shall not exceed 6.0μg/cm^2 for each specimen tested (list from NFPA 1994): 1. Acrolein 2. Acrylonitrile 3. Dimethyl sulfate 4. Ammonia (gas) 5. Chlorine (gas)
• Garment Level LERL-1 TIC Permeation Resistance	Test: Section 6.23, LERL-1 TIC Permeation Resistance Test • Specimens: Six swatches for each material and seam • Conditioning: Sample Preparation Applies NFPA 1991, Section 8.6, with NIJ modifications. • Chemical warfare agents (HD) and (GD) from NFPA 1994 • List of TICs from NFPA 1991 included to address clandestine labs NOTE: NFPA 1994 references ASTM Standard F739 (NIJ modification indicated below):	• Breakthrough detection time shall be ≥ one hour for each specimen calculated at a system detectable permeation rate of 0.10 μg/cm^2/min for liquid and gaseous TICS below: 1. Acetone 2. Acetonitrile 3. Anhydrous ammonia (gas) 4. 1,3-Butadiene (gas) 5. Carbon disulfide 6. Dichloromethane	N/A	N/A	N/A

109

CBRN Protective Ensemble Standard for Law Enforcement

Requirement	Test Method	LERL-1	LERL-2	LERL-3	LERL-4
	• Pouring liquid agent into a chamber next to a vertical swatch of protective material, so that it puddles up next to the fabric to measure how much breaks though • Liquid challenge concentration of 10 g/m² • Gas challenge concentrations specific to each gas • NIJ modification: swatch oriented in horizontal position allowing for a measurable quantity of challenge threat to be added to the swatch without having to flood the test cell	7. Diethyl amine 8. Dimethyl formamide 9. Ethyl acetate 10. Ethylene oxide (gas) 11. Hexane 12. Hydrogen chloride (gas) 13. Methanol 14. Methyl chloride (gas) 15. Nitrobenzene 16. Sodium hydroxide 17. Sulfuric acid 18. Tetrachloroethylene 19. Tetrahydrofuran 20. Toluene 21. Chlorine (gas)			
• Garment Level Viral Penetration Resistance	Test: Section 6.24, Viral Penetration Resistance Test • Specimens: Six swatches for each material and seam • Conditioning: Sample Preparation (except no gun lube; no sweat) • Applies ASTM Standard F1671, with NIJ modifications	• No penetration of Phi-X174 bacteriophage for one hour	• No penetration of Phi-X174 bacteriophage for one hour	• No penetration of Phi-X174 bacteriophage for one hour	• No penetration of Phi-X174 bacteriophage for one hour
• Garment Level Resistance to Liquid Penetration Under Pressure	Test: Section 6.25, Expulsion Test • Specimens: Six swatches for each material and seam • Conditioning: Sample Preparation • Applies ASTM Standard F1671, with NIJ modifications	• No penetration for one hour using MeS	• No penetration for one hour using MeS	• No penetration for one hour using MeS	• No penetration for one hour using MeS
• Garment Level Resistance to Liquid Penetration When Driven by Rain	Test: Section 6.26, Rain Cabinet Test • Specimens: Six swatches for each material and seam • Conditioning: Sample Preparation • Applies TOP 8-2-501, Section 4.3.7 with NIJ modifications	• No penetration for one hour using TEP simulant	• No penetration for one hour using TEP simulant	• No penetration for one hour using TEP simulant	• No penetration for one hour using TEP simulant

	Test				
Garment Level Tearing Strength	Test: Section 6.27, Tearing Strength Test • Specimens: Six swatches of woven outermost garment and hand protection element materials • Conditioning: Room Temperature Conditioning • Applies ASTM Standard D1424, with NIJ modifications	• Tear strength of not less than 50 N (11lbf)	• Tear strength of not less than 50 N (11lbf)	• Tear strength of not less than 50 N (11lbf)	• Tear strength of not less than 30 N (7 lbf)
Garment Level Cold Weather Performance	Test: Section 6.28, Cold Temperature Performance Test • Specimens: Six swatches • Conditioning: Room Temperature Conditioning • Applies ASTM Standard D2136, with NIJ modification of exposure temperature = -25°C	• Garment materials shall demonstrate no visible damage	• Garment materials shall demonstrate no visible damage	• Garment materials shall demonstrate no visible damage	• Garment materials shall demonstrate no visible damage
Garment Level Burst Strength	Test: Section 6.29, Burst Strength Test • Specimens: Six swatches of nonwoven outermost layer of garment and hand protection element materials • Conditioning: Room Temperature Conditioning • Applies ASTM Standard D3787	• Bursting strength of not less than 350N (79 lbf)	• Bursting strength of not less than 350N (79 lbf)	• Bursting strength of not less than 350N (79 lbf)	• Bursting strength of not less than 210N (47 lbf)
Garment Level Seam/Closure Breaking Strength	Test: Section 6.30, Seam/Closure Breaking Strength Test • Specimens: Seams and closures taken from finished garments with quantity as specified in ASTM Standard D1683 • Conditioning: Room Temperature Conditioning • Applies ASTM Standard D1683 with NIJ modifications	• Breaking strength of not less than 500N (112 lbf)	• Breaking strength of not less than 500N (112 lbf)	• Breaking strength of not less than 500N (112 lbf)	• Breaking strength of not less than 350N (79 lbf)

CBRN Protective Ensemble Standard for Law Enforcement

Requirement	Test				
• **Garment Level Cut Resistance of Woven Garment Materials**	Test: Section 6.31, Cut Resistance Test • Specimens: Five in each of the warp and fill directions • Conditioning: Room Temperature Conditioning • Applies ASTM Standard F1790, with NIJ modifications	• Cut resistance blade travel of not less than 25 mm (1 in) with a weight of 200 grams (7 oz)	• Cut resistance blade travel of not less than 25 mm (1 in) with a weight of 200 grams (7 oz)	• Cut resistance blade travel of not less than 25 mm (1 in) with a weight of 200 grams (7 oz)	• Cut resistance blade travel of not less than 25 mm (1 in) with a weight of 200 grams (7 oz)
• **Garment Level Puncture Resistance**	Test: Section 6.32, Puncture Resistance Test • Specimens: As specified in ASTM Standard F1342 • Conditioning: Room Temperature Conditioning • Applies ASTM Standard F1342, with NIJ modifications	• Puncture resistance of not less than 10 N (2lbf)	• Puncture resistance of not less than 10 N (2lbf)	• Puncture resistance of not less than 10 N (2lbf)	• Puncture resistance of not less than 10 N (2lbf)
• **Garment Level Total Heat Loss**	Test: Section 6.34, Total Heat Loss Test • Specimens: Six specimens of garment composites • Conditioning: Room Temperature Conditioning • Applies ASTM Standard F1868, with NIJ modifications	• Total heat loss ≥200 W/m²	• Total heat loss ≥250 W/m²	• Total heat loss ≥450 W/m²	• Total heat loss ≥450 W/m²
• **Garment Level Flame Resistance of Garment Composites**	Test: Section 6.40, Flame Resistance Test • Specimens: 10 in each of the warp and fill directions • Conditioning: Room Temperature Conditioning • Applies ASTM Standard D6413 with NIJ modifications	• Shall not have a char length of more than 100 mm (4 in) • Shall not have an afterflame of more than two seconds • Shall not melt or drip	N/A	N/A	N/A

112

• **Garment Level Flame Resistance of Zippers and Seam Sealing Materials**	Test: Section 6.40, Flame Resistance Test • Specimens: 10 • Conditioning: Room Temperature Conditioning • Applies ASTM Standard D6413 with NIJ modifications	When located on exterior of garment and not covered by flame-resistant material: • Shall not have a char length of more than 100 mm (4 in) • Shall not have an afterflame of more than two seconds • Shall not melt or drip	N/A	N/A
• **Garment Level Flame Impingement of Garment Components**	Test: Section 6.5, Flame Impingement Test • Specimens: As specified in ASTM F1358 • Conditioning: Room Temperature Conditioning • Applies ASTM F1358, with NIJ modifications	N/A	• Shall demonstrate no afterflame, no melt, and no drip after initial three-second exposure	• Shall demonstrate no afterflame, no melt, and no drip after initial three-second exposure
• **Garment Level Thermal Protective Performance**	Test: Section 6.35, Thermal Protective Performance Test • Specimens: Six • Conditioning: Room Temperature Conditioning • Applies NFPA 2112, Section 8.2, with NIJ modifications	• Shall have an average TPP of eight or greater	N/A	N/A
• **Garment Level Flame Protection**	Test: Section 6.21, Flash Fire Test • Specimens: Three complete ensembles, without respiratory protection • Conditioning: Ensemble Conditioning • Applies ASTM Standard F1930, with NIJ modifications	• Each specimen shall have an average percentage of TBSA of <25%, including 7% for the head	N/A	N/A
• **Garment Level Color/Visibility**	Test: Section 6.44, Color/Visibility Test Method • Specimens: Three each for each distinct color present on outer materials • Conditioning: Room Temperature Conditioning	• Shall have a Y brightness value <25 • Shall have an L* value < 55	• Shall have a Y brightness value <25 • Shall have an L* value <55	• Shall have a Y brightness value <25 • Shall have an L* value <55

Hand Protection Element Level Requirements:

Requirement	Test Method	LERL-1	LERL-2	LERL-3	LERL-4
• **Hand Protection Element Chemical Permeation Resistance**	Test: Section 6.22, Chemical Permeation Resistance Test • Specimens: Six swatches of each material and seam • Conditioning: Sample Preparation and conditioning at 32°C ± 3°C, RH 80% ± 5% for 24 hours immediately prior to testing • Applies ASTM Standard F739 with modifications	• HD: Cumulative permeation in one hour shall not exceed 4.0µg/cm² for each specimen tested • GD: Cumulative permeation in one hour shall not exceed 1.25µg/cm² for each specimen tested • For liquid and gaseous TICs listed below, cumulative permeation in one hour shall not exceed 6.0µg/cm² for each specimen tested (list from NFPA 1994): 1. Acrolein 2. Acrylonitrile 3. Dimethyl sulfate 4. Ammonia (gas) 5. Chlorine (gas)	• HD: Cumulative permeation in one hour shall not exceed 4.0µg/cm² for each specimen tested • GD: Cumulative permeation in one hour shall not exceed 1.25µg/cm² for each specimen tested • For liquid and gaseous TICs listed below, cumulative permeation in one hour shall not exceed 6.0µg/cm² for each specimen tested (list from NFPA 1994): 1. Acrolein 2. Acrylonitrile 3. Dimethyl sulfate 4. Ammonia (gas) 5. Chlorine (gas)	• HD: Cumulative permeation in one hour shall not exceed 4.0µg/cm² for each specimen tested • GD: Cumulative permeation in one hour shall not exceed 1.25µg/cm² for each specimen tested • For liquid and gaseous TICs listed below, cumulative permeation in one hour shall not exceed 6.0µg/cm² for each specimen tested (list from NFPA 1994): 1. Acrolein 2. Acrylonitrile 3. Dimethyl sulfate 4. Ammonia (gas) 5. Chlorine (gas)	• HD: Cumulative permeation in one hour shall not exceed 4.0µg/cm² for each specimen tested • GD: Cumulative permeation in one hour shall not exceed 1.25µg/cm² for each specimen tested • For liquid and gaseous TICs listed below, cumulative permeation in one hour shall not exceed 6.0µg/cm² for each specimen tested (list from NFPA 1994): 1. Acrolein 2. Acrylonitrile 3. Dimethyl sulfate 4. Ammonia (gas) 5. Chlorine (gas)
• **Hand Protection Element LERL-1 TIC Permeation Resistance**	Test: Section 6.23, LERL-1 TIC Permeation Resistance Test • Specimens: Six swatches for each material and seam • Conditioning: Sample Preparation • Applies NFPA 1991, Section 8.6, with NIJ modifications. • Chemical warfare agents (HD) and (GD) from NFPA 1994 • List of TICs from NFPA 1991 included to address	• Breakthrough detection time shall be ≥ one hour for each specimen calculated at a system detectable permeation rate of 0.10 µg/cm²/min for liquid and gaseous TICS below: 1. Acetone 2. Acetonitrile 3. Anhydrous ammonia (gas)	N/A	N/A	N/A

CBRN Protective Ensemble Standard for Law Enforcement

Requirement	Test Method	LERL-1	LERL-2	LERL-3	LERL-4
	clandestine labs **NOTE:** NFPA 1994 references ASTM Standard F739 (NIJ modification indicated below): • Pouring liquid agent into a chamber next to a vertical swatch of protective material, so that it puddles up next to the fabric to measure how much breaks though • Liquid challenge concentration of 10 g/m^2 • Gas challenge concentrations specific to each gas • NIJ modification: swatch oriented in horizontal position allowing for a measurable quantity of challenge threat to be added to the swatch without having to flood the test cell	4. 1,3-Butadiene (gas) 5. Carbon disulfide 6. Dichloromethane 7. Diethyl amine 8. Dimethyl formamide 9. Ethyl acetate 10. Ethylene oxide (gas) 11. Hexane 12. Hydrogen chloride (gas) 13. Methanol 14. Methyl chloride (gas) 15. Nitrobenzene 16. Sodium hydroxide 17. Sulfuric acid 18. Tetrachloroethylene 19. Tetrahydrofuran 20. Toluene 21. Chlorine (gas)			
• **Hand Protection Element Viral Penetration Resistance**	Test: Section 6.24, Viral Penetration Resistance Test • Specimens: Six swatches for each material and seam • Conditioning: Sample Preparation (except no gun lube; no sweat) • Applies ASTM Standard F1671, with NIJ modifications	• No penetration of Phi-X174 bacteriophage for one hour	• No penetration of Phi-X174 bacteriophage for one hour	• No penetration of Phi-X174 bacteriophage for one hour	• No penetration of Phi-X174 bacteriophage for one hour
• **Hand Protection Element Resistance to Liquid Penetration Under Pressure**	Test: Section 6.25, Expulsion Test • Specimens: Six swatches for each material and seam • Conditioning: Sample Preparation • Applies ASTM Standard F1671, with NIJ modifications	• No penetration for one hour using MeS	• No penetration for one hour using MeS	• No penetration for one hour using MeS	• No penetration for one hour using MeS

Hand Protection Element Resistance to Liquid Penetration When Driven by Rain	Test: Section 6.26, Rain Cabinet Test • Specimens: Six swatches for each material and seam • Conditioning: Sample Preparation • Applies TOP 8-2-501, Section 4.3.7 with NIJ modifications	• No penetration for one hour using TEP simulant	• No penetration for one hour using TEP simulant	• No penetration for one hour using TEP simulant	• No penetration for one hour using TEP simulant
Hand Protection Element Cut Resistance	Test: Section 6.31, Cut Resistance Test • Specimens: Five in each of the warp and fill directions • Conditioning: Room Temperature Conditioning • Applies ASTM Standard F1790, with NIJ modifications	• Cut resistance blade travel of not less than 25 mm (1 in) with a weight of 200 grams (7 oz)	• Cut resistance blade travel of not less than 25 mm (1 in) with a weight of 200 grams (7 oz)	• Cut resistance blade travel of not less than 25 mm (1 in) with a weight of 200 grams (7 oz)	• Cut resistance blade travel of not less than 25 mm (1 in) with a weight of 200 grams (7 oz)
Hand Protection Element Puncture Resistance	Test: Section 6.32, Puncture Resistance Test • Specimens: As specified in ASTM Standard F1342 • Conditioning: Room Temperature Conditioning • Applies ASTM Standard F1342, with NIJ modifications	• Puncture resistance of not less than 15 N (4 lbf)	• Puncture resistance of not less than 15 N (4 lbf)	• Puncture resistance of not less than 15 N (4 lbf)	• Puncture resistance of not less than 15 N (4 lbf)
Hand Protection Element Cold Weather Performance	Test: Section 6.28, Cold Temperature Performance Test • Specimens: Six swatches • Conditioning: Room Temperature Conditioning • Applies ASTM Standard D2136, with NIJ modification of exposure temperature = -25°C	• Hand protection element materials shall demonstrate no visible damage	• Hand protection element materials shall demonstrate no visible damage	• Hand protection element materials shall demonstrate no visible damage	• Hand protection element materials shall demonstrate no visible damage

	Test				
Hand Protection Element Grip	• Test: Section 6.38, Grip Test • Applies NFPA 1951, with NIJ modifications • Five pairs each in both the largest and smallest sizes conditioned per NFPA 1951, 8.1.2 • Five pairs each in both the largest and smallest sizes conditioned per NFPA 1951, 8.1.2 and 8.1.7 • Conditioning: As defined above	• Shall have a weight-pulling capacity of not less than 95% of bare-handed control values	• Shall have a weight-pulling capacity of not less than 95% of bare-handed control values	• Shall have a weight-pulling capacity of not less than 95% of bare-handed control values	• Shall have a weight-pulling capacity of not less than 95% of bare-handed control values
Hand Protection Element Seam/Closure Breaking Strength	• Test: Section 6.30, Seam/Closure Breaking Strength Test • Specimens: Seams and closures taken from finished garments with quantity as specified in ASTM Standard D1683 • Conditioning: Room Temperature Conditioning • Applies ASTM Standard D1683 with NIJ modifications	• Breaking strength of not less than 500 N (112 lbf)	• Breaking strength of not less than 500 N (112 lbf)	• Breaking strength of not less than 500 N (112 lbf)	• Breaking strength of not less than 350 N (79 lbf)
Hand Protection Element Burst Strength	• Test: Section 6.29, Burst Strength Test • Specimens: Six swatches of nonwoven outermost layer of garment and hand protection element materials • Conditioning: Room Temperature Conditioning Applies ASTM Standard D3787	• Bursting strength of not less than 350 N (79 lbf)	• Bursting strength of not less than 350 N (79 lbf)	• Bursting strength of not less than 350 N (79 lbf)	• Bursting strength of not less than 210 N (47 lbf)
Hand Protection Element Tearing Strength	• Test: Section 6.27, Tearing Strength Test • Specimens: Six swatches of woven outermost garment and hand protection element materials • Conditioning: Room Temperature Conditioning Applies ASTM Standard D1424,	• Tear strength of not less than 50 N (11lbf)	• Tear strength of not less than 50 N (11lbf)	• Tear strength of not less than 50 N (11lbf)	• Tear strength of not less than 30 N (7 lbf)

117

Element	Test / Method				
• **Hand Protection Element Flame Resistance**	with NIJ modifications Test: Section 6.40, Flame Resistance Test • Specimens: 10 • Conditioning: Room Temperature Conditioning • Applies ASTM Standard D6413 with NIJ modifications	• Shall not have a char length of more than 100 mm (4 in) • Shall not have an afterflame of more than two seconds • Shall not melt or drip	N/A	N/A	N/A
• **Hand Protection Element Flame Impingement**	Test: Section 6.5, Flame Impingement Test • Specimens: As specified in ASTM F1358 • Conditioning: Room Temperature Conditioning • Applies ASTM F1358, with NIJ modifications	N/A	• Shall demonstrate no afterflame, not melt, and no drip after initial three-second exposure	• Shall demonstrate no afterflame, not melt, and no drip after initial three-second exposure	• Shall demonstrate no afterflame, not melt, and no drip after initial three-second exposure
• **Hand Protection Element Thermal Protective Performance**	Test: Section 6.35, Thermal Protective Performance Test • Specimens: Six • Conditioning: Room Temperature Conditioning • Applies NFPA 2112, Section 8.2, with NIJ modifications	• Shall have an average TPP of eight or greater	N/A	N/A	N/A
• **Hand Protection Element Color/Visibility**	Test: Section 6.44, Color/Visibility Test Method • Specimens: Three each for each distinct color present on outer materials • Conditioning: Room Temperature Conditioning	• Shall have a Y brightness value < 25 • Shall have an L* value < 55	• Shall have a Y brightness value < 25 • Shall have an L* value < 55	• Shall have a Y brightness value < 25 • Shall have an L* value < 55	• Shall have a Y brightness value < 25 • Shall have an L* value < 55

Foot Protection Element Level Requirements:

Requirement	Test Method	LERL-1	LERL-2	LERL-3	LERL-4
• Foot Protection Element Level Chemical Permeation Resistance	Test: Section 6.22, Chemical Permeation Resistance Test • Specimens: Six swatches of each material and seam • Conditioning: Sample Preparation and conditioning at $32°C \pm 3°C$, RH $80\% \pm 5\%$ for 24 hours immediately prior to testing • Applies ASTM Standard F739 with modifications	• HD: Cumulative permeation in one hour shall not exceed $4.0\mu g/cm^2$ for each specimen tested • GD: Cumulative permeation in one hour shall not exceed $1.25\mu g/cm^2$ for each specimen tested • For liquid and gaseous TICs listed below, cumulative permeation in one hour shall not exceed $6.0\mu g/cm^2$ for each specimen tested (list from NFPA 1994): 1. Acrolein 2. Acrylonitrile 3. Dimethyl sulfate 4. Ammonia (gas) 5. Chlorine (gas)	• HD: Cumulative permeation in one hour shall not exceed $4.0\mu g/cm^2$ for each specimen tested • GD: Cumulative permeation in one hour shall not exceed $1.25\mu g/cm^2$ for each specimen tested • For liquid and gaseous TICs listed below, cumulative permeation in one hour shall not exceed $6.0\mu g/cm^2$ for each specimen tested (list from NFPA 1994): 6. Acrolein 7. Acrylonitrile 8. Dimethyl sulfate 9. Ammonia (gas) 10. Chlorine (gas)	• HD: Cumulative permeation in one hour shall not exceed $4.0\mu g/cm^2$ for each specimen tested • GD: Cumulative permeation in one hour shall not exceed $1.25\mu g/cm^2$ for each specimen tested • For liquid and gaseous TICs listed below, cumulative permeation in one hour shall not exceed $6.0\mu g/cm^2$ for each specimen tested (list from NFPA 1994): 11. Acrolein 12. Acrylonitrile 13. Dimethyl sulfate 14. Ammonia (gas) 15. Chlorine (gas)	• HD: Cumulative permeation in one hour shall not exceed $4.0\mu g/cm^2$ for each specimen tested • GD: Cumulative permeation in one hour shall not exceed $1.25\mu g/cm^2$ for each specimen tested • For liquid and gaseous TICs listed below, cumulative permeation in one hour shall not exceed $6.0\mu g/cm^2$ for each specimen tested (list from NFPA 1994): 16. Acrolein 17. Acrylonitrile 18. Dimethyl sulfate 19. Ammonia (gas) 20. Chlorine (gas)
• Foot Protection Element LERL-1 TIC Permeation Resistance	Test: Section 6.23, LERL-1 TIC Permeation Resistance Test • Specimens: Six swatches for each material and seam • Conditioning: Sample Preparation • Applies NFPA 1991, Section 8.6, with NIJ modifications. • Chemical warfare agents (HD) and (GD) from NFPA 1994 • List of TICs from NFPA 1991 included to address clandestine labs **NOTE:** NFPA 1994 references	• Breakthrough detection time shall be $\geq$ one hour for each specimen calculated at a system detectable permeation rate of $0.10\ \mu g/cm^2/min$ for liquid and gaseous TICS below: 1. Acetone 2. Acetonitrile 3. Anhydrous ammonia (gas) 4. 1,3-Butadiene (gas) 5. Carbon disulfide	• N/A	• N/A	• N/A

CBRN Protective Ensemble Standard for Law Enforcement

Requirement	Test Method	LERL-1	LERL-2	LERL-3	LERL-4
	ASTM Standard F739 (NIJ modification indicated below): • Pouring liquid agent into a chamber next to a vertical swatch of protective material, so that it puddles up next to the fabric to measure how much breaks though • Liquid challenge concentration of 10 g/m² • Gas challenge concentrations specific to each gas • NIJ modification: swatch oriented in horizontal position allowing for a measurable quantity of challenge threat to be added to the swatch without having to flood the test cell	6. Dichloromethane 7. Diethyl amine 8. Dimethyl formamide 9. Ethyl acetate 10. Ethylene oxide (gas) 11. Hexane 12. Hydrogen chloride (gas) 13. Methanol 14. Methyl chloride (gas) 15. Nitrobenzene 16. Sodium hydroxide 17. Sulfuric acid 18. Tetrachloroethylene 19. Tetrahydrofuran 20. Toluene 21. Chlorine (gas)			
• **Foot Protection Element Viral Penetration Resistance**	Test: Section 6.24, Viral Penetration Resistance Test • Specimens: Six swatches for each material and seam • Conditioning: Sample Preparation (except no gun lube; no sweat) • Applies ASTM Standard F1671, with NIJ modifications	• No penetration of Phi-X174 bacteriophage for one hour	• No penetration of Phi-X174 bacteriophage for one hour	• No penetration of Phi-X174 bacteriophage for one hour	• No penetration of Phi-X174 bacteriophage for one hour
• **Foot Protection Element Resistance to Liquid Penetration Under Pressure**	Test: Section 6.25, Expulsion Test • Specimens: Six swatches for each material and seam • Conditioning: Sample Preparation • Applies ASTM Standard F1671, with NIJ modifications	• No penetration for one hour using MeS	• No penetration for one hour using MeS	• No penetration for one hour using MeS	• No penetration for one hour using MeS

	Test				
Foot Protection Element Resistance to Liquid Penetration When Driven By Rain	Test: Section 6.26, Rain Cabinet Test • Specimens: Six swatches for each material and seam • Conditioning: Sample Preparation • Applies TOP 8-2-501, Section 4.3.7 with NIJ modifications	• No penetration for one hour using TEP simulant	• No penetration for one hour using TEP simulant	• No penetration for one hour using TEP simulant	• No penetration for one hour using TEP simulant
Foot Protection Element Cut Resistance	Test: Section 6.31, Cut Resistance Test • Specimens: Five in each of the warp and fill directions • Conditioning: Room Temperature Conditioning • Applies ASTM Standard F1790, with NIJ modifications	• Cut resistance blade travel of not less than 25 mm (1 in) with a weight of 200 grams (7 oz)	• Cut resistance blade travel of not less than 25 mm (1 in) with a weight of 200 grams (7 oz)	• Cut resistance blade travel of not less than 25 mm (1 in) with a weight of 200 grams (7 oz)	• Cut resistance blade travel of not less than 25 mm (1 in) with a weight of 200 grams (7 oz)
Foot Protection Element Puncture Resistance	Test: Section 6.32, Puncture Resistance Test • Specimens: As specified in ASTM Standard F1342 • Conditioning: Room Temperature Conditioning • Applies ASTM Standard F1342, with NIJ modifications	• Puncture resistance of not less than 36 N (8 lbf)	• Puncture resistance of not less than 36 N (8 lbf)	• Puncture resistance of not less than 36 N (8 lbf)	• Puncture resistance of not less than 36 N (8 lbf)
Foot Protection Element Abrasion Resistance	Test: Section 6.39, Abrasion Resistance Test • Specimens: 10 specimens from foot protection element • Conditioning: Room Temperature Conditioning • Applies ASTM Standard D1630, with NIJ modifications	• Each specimen shall have an abrasion-resistance rating of not less than 65	• Each specimen shall have an abrasion-resistance rating of not less than 65	• Each specimen shall have an abrasion-resistance rating of not less than 65	• Each specimen shall have an abrasion-resistance rating of not less than 65

CBRN Protective Ensemble Standard for Law Enforcement

Foot Protection Element Slip Resistance	Test: Section 6.42, Slip Resistance Test • Specimens: Three footwear specimens or footwear cover specimens • Conditioning: Room Temperature Conditioning • Applies ASTM Standard F489 in a dry and a wet condition	• Each specimen shall have a static coefficient of 0.75 or greater	• Each specimen shall have a static coefficient of 0.75 or greater	• Each specimen shall have a static coefficient of 0.75 or greater	• Each specimen shall have a static coefficient of 0.75 or greater
Foot Protection Element Flame Resistance	Test: Section 6.40, Flame Resistance Test • Specimens: 10 • Conditioning: Room Temperature Conditioning • Applies ASTM Standard D6413 with NIJ modifications	• Shall not have a char length of more than 100 mm (4 in) • Shall not have an afterflame of more than two seconds • Shall not melt or drip	N/A	N/A	N/A
Foot Protection Element Flame Impingement	Test: Section 6.5, Flame Impingement Test • Specimens: As specified in ASTM F1358 • Conditioning: Room Temperature Conditioning • Applies ASTM F1358, with NIJ modifications	N/A	• Shall not have an afterflame • Shall demonstrate no afterflame, no melt and no drip after initial three-second exposure	• Shall not have an afterflame • Shall demonstrate no afterflame, no melt and no drip after initial three-second exposure	• Shall not have an afterflame • Shall demonstrate no afterflame, no melt and no drip after initial three-second exposure
Foot Protection Element Thermal Protective Performance	Test: Section 6.35, Thermal Protective Performance Test • Specimens: Six • Conditioning: Room Temperature Conditioning • Applies NFPA 2112, Section 8.2, with NIJ modifications	• Shall have an average TPP of 8 or greater	N/A	N/A	N/A
Foot Protection Element Color/Visibility	Test: Section 6.44, Color/Visibility Test Method • Specimens: Three each for each distinct color present on outer materials • Conditioning: Room Temperature Conditioning	• Shall have a Y brightness value <25 • Shall have an L* value < 55	• Shall have a Y brightness value <25 • Shall have an L* value < 55	• Shall have a Y brightness value <25 • Shall have an L* value < 55	• Shall have a Y brightness value <25 • Shall have an L* value < 55

ANNEX D. Summary of Placement of Labeling and Information/Compliant CBRN Protective Ensemble Models

The following tables summarize requirements as to the placement of labeling and information on or with the ensemble and its elements.[20]

Table 10. Ensemble With Attached Hand and Foot Protection Elements: Placement of Required Labeling and Information

Ensemble			
• User information (to be provided by the ensemble manufacturer with each individual ensemble) • Technical Data Package(to be provided by the ensemble manufacturer upon request)			
Garment Element	**Foot Protection Element**	**Hand Protection Element**	**Respiratory Protection Element**[21]
• Ensemble product label • Ensemble model compliance statement	• No separate label or compliance statement	• No separate label or compliance statement	• Not addressed by this NIJ standard

Table 11. Ensemble With Detached Hand and Foot Protection Elements: Placement of Required Labeling and Information

Ensemble			
• User information (to be provided by the ensemble manufacturer with each individual ensemble) • Technical Data Package (to be provided by the ensemble manufacturer on request)			
Garment Element	**Foot Protection Element**	**Hand Protection Element**	**Respiratory Protection Element**[22]
• Ensemble product label • Ensemble model compliance statement	• Foot protection element product label • No separate compliance statement	• Hand protection element product label • No separate compliance statement	• Not addressed by this NIJ standard

---

[20] Please refer to the text of this NIJ standard (in particular, Chapter 7) for complete details. Should there be any discrepancy between that text and this summary annex, the former controls.

[21] The technical data package and user information must specify the manufacturer and specific model(s) of respiratory protection successfully tested with the ensemble model and associated interface considerations. Labeling of respiratory protection is not addressed by this NIJ standard.

[22] The technical data package and user information must specify the manufacturer and specific model(s) of respiratory protection successfully tested with the ensemble model and associated interface considerations. Labeling of respiratory protection is not addressed by this NIJ standard.

About the Law Enforcement and Corrections Standards and Testing Program

The National Institute of Justice (NIJ) Standards and Testing Program is sponsored by the NIJ Office of Science and Technology within the U.S. Department of Justice, Office of Justice Programs. The program responds to provisions in the Homeland Security Act of 2002 that authorize the NIJ Office of Science and Technology to establish and maintain performance standards (in accordance with the National Technology Transfer and Advancement Act of 1995) for law enforcement technologies that may be used by federal, state and local law enforcement agencies, and to test and evaluate those technologies. The Homeland Security Act of 2002 also authorizes the NIJ Office of Science and Technology to establish and maintain a program to certify, validate and mark or otherwise recognize law enforcement technology products that conform to the standards mentioned above.

The NIJ Standards and Testing Program works to identify the needs of state and local criminal justice system practitioners for equipment standards and test protocols, develops voluntary performance standards for specific criminal justice tools and technologies, establishes conformity assessment requirements for demonstrating that commercially available equipment conforms to those standards, and publishes listings of product models that have been tested through one or more specified organizations and found to comply with the standards. The standards development process begins with the operational needs and requirements of practitioners in the field being defined, and, based on those needs, the standards are developed principally by a special technical committee led by criminal justice practitioners and including testing and conformity assessment experts, other technical experts, federal partners and members from practitioner stakeholder organizations. Manufacturers, vendors and other interested parties are provided with an opportunity to review and comment on draft standards prior to their publication.

As indicated above, all NIJ standards developed through the Standards and Testing Program are voluntary standards. There is no requirement or obligation for manufacturers, law enforcement agencies or others to follow or adopt these voluntary law enforcement technology equipment standards. The primary intent of these standards is to provide the end user of a model of equipment found to be compliant with a particular standard with performance information on key equipment characteristics, provide a level of confidence in that particular model's fitness for use in specified circumstances and allow comparison of product models based on standardized testing methods and performance requirements. These standards do not specify a particular solution but rather define what a potential solution must accomplish. The ultimate goal is to help ensure to the degree possible that law enforcement technology equipment is safe, reliable and effective.

Publications related to the Standards and Testing Program, including the voluntary standards and associated documents, are available at no charge through the National Law Enforcement and Corrections Technology Center-National (NLECTC-National) and also are available online at http://www.nij.gov/standards and http://www.justnet.org. To request a document or additional information, please call (800) 248-2742 or (301) 519-5060, or send an e-mail to asknlectc@nlectc.org.

Users of NIJ standards are advised to check with http://www.nij.gov/standards on a regular basis to determine whether a particular law enforcement technology equipment standard has been revised or superseded, or the compliance status of a particular model has changed.

www.ingramcontent.com/pod-product-compliance
Lightning Source LLC
Chambersburg PA
CBHW080255180526
45167CB00006B/2543